ELIZABETH THE QUEEN

By Maxwell Anderson

YOU WHO HAVE DREAMS (*Poems*)
SATURDAY'S CHILDREN
OUTSIDE LOOKING IN

In collaboration with
Lawrence Stallings
WHAT PRICE GLORY

ELIZABETH THE QUEEN
A Play in Three Acts

BY

MAXWELL ANDERSON

LONGMANS, GREEN AND CO.
LONDON · NEW YORK · TORONTO
1931

LONGMANS, GREEN AND CO.

55 FIFTH AVENUE, NEW YORK
221 EAST 20TH STREET, CHICAGO
88 TREMONT STREET, BOSTON
128 UNIVERSITY AVENUE, TORONTO

LONGMANS, GREEN AND CO. LTD.

39 PATERNOSTER ROW, E C 4, LONDON
6 OLD COURT HOUSE STREET, CALCUTTA
53 NICOL ROAD, BOMBAY
36A MOUNT ROAD, MADRAS

ANDERSON
ELIZABETH THE QUEEN

First Edition November 1930
Reprinted January 1931
April 1931

MADE IN THE UNITED STATES OF AMERICA

822

TO
M. H. A.

ELIZABETH THE QUEEN

CHARACTERS

ELIZABETH THE QUEEN

ACT ONE

SCENE I

SCENE: *An entrance hall before a council chamber in the palace at Whitehall. The entrance to the council room is closed and four* GUARDS *with halberds stand at either side. A small door at the left of the entrance is also shut. It is early morning. The guards stand immobile.*

FIRST GUARD

The sun's out again, and it's guineas to pounds the earl comes back this morning.

SECOND GUARD

I'll be glad of it, for one. You get nothing but black looks about the court when he's away.

FIRST GUARD

You'll get little else now he's back, my bully. They quarrelled too far for mending, this time.

THIRD GUARD

Tut! They quarrel no more than the cock with the hen. The earl's been sick.

3

FIRST GUARD

Sick of the queen's displeasure. It's a disease a favorite
can die of, and many have.

FOURTH GUARD

He's no sicker of her displeasure than she of his, if a man
may judge. Once the earl's gone there's no dancing, no
plays, no feasting . . . nothing to do nights but sleep.
The very scullery-maids grow cold, and go to bed alone;
like the queen.

FIRST GUARD

There are some even a scullery-maid would seldom kiss,
save in moments of great excitement. Poor Wat looks
forward to feast nights.

FOURTH GUARD

I've had my luck.

FIRST GUARD

You've had what was coming to you. Mucklemouth
Jean, of the back kitchen.

FOURTH GUARD

You'd have been glad of her yourself if you could have
had her.

FIRST GUARD

Consider, man. She may not have been true. When
she wouldn't play with you, mayhap she was playing
with somebody else. And if the queen could live without her Earl of Essex, it may have been because Sir
Walter had a new suit of silver armor.

THIRD GUARD

And there's a handsome man.

FOURTH GUARD

God defend me from speaking lightly of the queen!

FIRST GUARD

Eh? God defend you? Let no man accuse me of speaking lightly of the queen, nor of any other woman . . . unless she be a light woman, in which case, God defend me, I will speak lightly of her if I choose.

THIRD GUARD

What say you of the queen?

FIRST GUARD

Of the queen? I say she is well-known to be the virgin queen, I say no more.

SECOND GUARD

But do you think she is a virgin?

FIRST GUARD

She has doubtless been a virgin, bully, for all women have been virgins, but the question is: First, when . . . and, second, where?

SECOND GUARD

Where?

FIRST GUARD

Where, bully, where?

THIRD GUARD

Would you not say, in the proper place?

FIRST GUARD

No. I would not say in the proper place. Because it is hard to say if there is a proper place wherein to be a

virgin . . . unless it be in church, and, God defend
me, I do not go to church.

SECOND GUARD

You do not go to church ?

FIRST GUARD

No, for my sins, I do not go to church . . . or, if you
like, I do not go to church for my sins.

SECOND GUARD

Does it follow that the church is a proper place for
virgins ?

FIRST GUARD

It does.   Did I not tell you I do not go there for my
sins ?

FOURTH GUARD

They say the queen's getting to be an old woman but I
swear she looks younger than my wife, whom I married
a young thing, six years come Easter.

THIRD GUARD

It would age a girl fast, just the look of you.

FIRST GUARD

As for the queen, powder and paint accounts for some
of it.   To say nothing of the earl.   A young lover will
do much for a lady's face.

FOURTH GUARD

Now God defend me. . .

Aye, aye . . . God defend poor Wat.

[*A* NOBLEMAN *enters in silver armor. It is* SIR WALTER RALEIGH, *no other.*]

RALEIGH

Has the queen come forth yet ?

FIRST GUARD

No, Sir Walter.

RALEIGH

The Earl of Essex . . . is he here ?

FIRST GUARD

No, my lord.

RALEIGH

When he comes send me word. I shall be in the north corridor. [*He turns.*]

FIRST GUARD

Good, my lord.

[PENELOPE GRAY *comes in from the right, passing through.*]

RALEIGH

[*Meeting her*] Greetings, lady, from my heart.

PENELOPE

Good-morrow, lord, from my soul.

RALEIGH

I take my oath in your face that you are rushing to the window to witness the arrival of my lord of Essex.

PENELOPE

And in your teeth I swear I am on no such errand . . .
but only to see the sun-rise.

RALEIGH

The sun has been up this hour, my dear.

PENELOPE

The more reason to hurry, gracious knight.

RALEIGH

Do you think to pull the bag over my head so easily,
Penelope ?   On a day when the earl returns every petti-
coat in the palace is hung with an eye to pleasing him.
Yours not the least.

PENELOPE

I deny him thrice.

RALEIGH

I relinquish you, lady.   Run, run to the window !   He
will be here and you will miss him !

PENELOPE

Is there a lady would run from Sir Walter in his silver
suiting ?   Since the sun is up . . . I have no errand.

RALEIGH

Is there no limit to a woman's deception, wench ?
Would you go so far as to appear pleased if I kissed you ?

PENELOPE

And no deception.   [*He kisses her.*]   I call the Gods
to witness . . . did I not blush prettily ?

RALEIGH

And meant it not at all. Tell me, did the queen send you to look out the casement for news of her Essex, or did you come at the prompting of your heart ?

PENELOPE

Shall I tell you the truth ?

RALEIGH

Verily.

PENELOPE

The truth is I cannot answer.

RALEIGH

Both, then ?

PENELOPE

Both or one or neither.

RALEIGH

Fie on the baggage.

PENELOPE

Is it not a virtue to be close-mouthed in the queen's service ?

RALEIGH

If you kept the rest of your person as close as your mouth what a paragon of virtue you would be !

PENELOPE

Indeed, my lord, I am.

RALEIGH

Indeed, my lady ? Have there not been certain deeds on dark nights ?

PENELOPE

Sh !   Under the rose.

RALEIGH

Meaning under covers. . .

PENELOPE

Fie on my lord, to make me out a strumpet !

RALEIGH

It is my manner of wooing, fair maid !   I woo by sug-
gestion of images. . .

PENELOPE

Like small boys on the closet wall. . .

RALEIGH

Like a soldier. . .

PENELOPE

Aye, a veteran . . . of encounters. . .

RALEIGH

I will have you yet, my love; I will take lessons from
this earl. . .

PENELOPE

Take this lesson from me, my lord: You must learn
to desire what you would have.   Much wanting makes
many a maid a wanton.   You want me not . . . nor I
you.   You wear your silver for a queen.
[*A* CAPTAIN *enters from the left.*]

CAPTAIN

Good-morrow, Sir Walter.   Is the queen still under
canopy ?

RALEIGH

I know not.

CAPTAIN

The earl is here and would see her.

RALEIGH

Bid him hurry if he wishes to find her abed as usual.

PENELOPE

She is dressed and stirring, captain, and awaits my lord.

RALEIGH

And many another fair maid awaits him likewise, captain. Take him that message from me. Run, girl, run. Tell the queen.
[*The* CAPTAIN *goes out left.*]

PENELOPE

[*Going*] You make yourself so easily disliked. [*She goes right.* CECIL *enters, passing her.*]

CECIL

He is here ?

RALEIGH

So. The heavenly boy, clad in the regalia of the sun, even now extracts his gallant foot from his golden stirrup and makes shift to descend from his heaving charger. Acclamation lifts in every voice, tears well to every eye . . . with the exception of mine, perhaps, and yours, I hope. . .

CECIL

I am at a pass to welcome him, myself.   This Elizabeth

of ours can be difficult on her good days . . . and there
have been no good ones lately.

[*Two* MEN-AT-ARMS *enter with silver armor in their
arms.*]

RALEIGH

And what is all this, sirrah ?

FIRST MAN

Armor, my lord.

RALEIGH

For whom ?

FIRST MAN

We know not.

RALEIGH

Now by the ten thousand holy names ! Am I mistaken, Robert, or is this armor much like my own ?

CECIL

Very like, I should say. Is it sterling ?

RALEIGH

And the self-same pattern. Has the earl gone lunatic ?

CECIL

He means to outshine you, perhaps.

RALEIGH

Has it come to this ? Do I set the style for Essex ?
That would be a mad trick, to dress himself like me !
[BACON *appears in the doorway at right.*]
What do you know of this, Sir Francis ?

BACON

Greeks, my lord, bearing gifts.

RALEIGH

To hell with your Greeks ! The devil damn him !
This is some blackguardry !
[*Two more* MEN-AT-ARMS *enter, carrying armor.*]
There's more of it ! Good God, it comes in bales !
I say, who's to wear this, sirrah ? Who is it for ?
[ESSEX *enters from corridor between the two files of soldiers, pushing them aside as he does so, and crosses to right of* RALEIGH, *speaking as he enters.*]

ESSEX

Their name is legion, Sir Walter. Happily met !
Felicitations on your effulgence, sir !
You're more splendid than I had imagined ! News came
    of your silver
Even in my retreat ! I was ill, and I swear it cured me !
You should have heard the compliments I've heard
Passed on you ! Sir Walter's in silver ! The world's
    outdone
They said — the moon out-mooned. He gleams down
    every corridor
And every head's turned after him. The queen
Herself has admired it — the design — the workman-
    ship !
There's nothing like it this side of Heaven's streets.
And I said to myself — the great man — this is what we
    have needed —
More silver everywhere — oceans of silver !
Sir Walter has set the style, the world will follow.
So I sent for the silver-smiths, and by their sweat
Here's for you, lads, tailored to every man's measure —
Shall Raleigh wear silver alone ? Why, no,
The whole court shall go argent !

RALEIGH

Take care, my lord.
I bear insults badly.

ESSEX

And where are you insulted ?
For the queen's service you buy you a silver armor.
In the queen's service I buy you a dozen more.
A gift, my friends, each man to own his own,
As you own yours.   What insult ?

RALEIGH

Have your laugh,
Let the queen and court laugh with you !   Since you are
    envious
You may have my suit.   I had not thought even Essex
Bore so petty a mind.

ESSEX

I misunderstood you
Perhaps, Sir Walter.   I had supposed you donned
Silver for our queen, but I was mistaken . . .
Keep these all for yourself. The men shall have
    others . . .
Some duller color.

RALEIGH

I have borne much from you
Out of regard for the queen, my lord of Essex.

ESSEX

And I from you.
By God . . .

CECIL

You have forgotten, Sir Walter,
A certain appointment . . .

RALEIGH

And you will bear more, by Heaven ! . . .

CECIL

He is going to the queen,
Remember.   And we have an errand.

ESSEX

You presume to protect me,
Master Secretary ?

CECIL

I protect you both, and our mistress.
There can be no quarrelling here.

RALEIGH

That's very true.   Let us go.
[CECIL *and* RALEIGH *go out right.*]

BACON

And this armor ?   What becomes of it ?

ESSEX

I have given it.
Would you have me take it back ?

BACON

There has seldom been
A man so little wise, so headstrong, but he
Could sometimes see how necessary it is

To keep friends and not make enemies at court.
But you . . . God knows.

ESSEX

Let him make friends with me.
He may need friends himself.
[*To the* GUARDS]
These are your armors.
Keep them, wear them, sell them, whatever you like . . .
Or your captain directs you.

FIRST GUARD

We thank you.
[*They retire to examine the armor.*]

BACON

You are going to the queen ?

ESSEX

Yes.   God help us both !

BACON

Then hear me a moment. . .

ESSEX

Speak, schoolmaster,
I knew it was coming.   You've been quiet too long.

BACON

Listen to me this once, and listen this once
To purpose, my lord, or it may hardly be worth
My while ever to give you advice again
Or for you to take it.   You have enough on your hands
Without quarrelling with Raleigh.   You have quarrelled
   with the queen
Against my judgment. . .

ESSEX

God and the devil ! Can a man
Quarrel on order or avoid a quarrel at will ?

BACON

Why certainly, if he knows his way.

ESSEX

Not I.

BACON

You quarrelled with her, because she wished to keep
peace
And you wanted war. . .

ESSEX

We are at war with Spain !
But such a silly, frightened, womanish war
As only a woman would fight. . .

BACON

She is a woman and fights a womanish war;
But ask yourself one question and answer it
Honestly, dear Essex, and perhaps you will see then
Why I speak sharply. You are my friend and patron.
Where you gain I gain . . . where you lose I lose . . .
And I see you riding straight to a fall today . . .
And I'd rather your neck weren't broken.

ESSEX

Ask myself
What question ?

BACON

Ask yourself what you want:
To retain the favor of the queen, remain

Her favorite, keep all that goes with this,
Or set yourself against her and trust your fortune
To popular favor ?

ESSEX

I'll not answer that.

BACON

Then . . . I have done.

ESSEX

Forgive me, dear friend, forgive me.
I have been ill, and this silly jackanapes
Of a Raleigh angers me with his silver mountings
Till I forget who's my friend.   You know my answer
In regard to the queen.   I must keep her favor.
Only it makes me mad to see all this . . .
This utter mismanagement, when a man's hand and
    brain
Are needed and cannot be used.

BACON

Let me answer for you;
You are not forthright with yourself.   The queen
Fights wars with tergiversation and ambiguities . . .
You wish to complete your record as general,
Crush Spain, subdue Ireland, make a name like Cæsar's,
Climb to the pinnacle of fame.   Take care.
You are too popular already. You have
Won at Cadiz, caught the people's hearts,
Caught their voices till the streets ring your name
Whenever you pass.   You are loved better than
The queen.   That is your danger.   She will not suffer

A subject to eclipse her; she cannot suffer it.
Make no mistake. She will not.

ESSEX

And I must wait,
Bite my nails in a corner, let her lose to Spain,
Keep myself back for policy ?

BACON

Even so.

ESSEX

I come of better blood than Elizabeth.
My name was among the earls around King John
Under the oak. What the nobles have taught a king
A noble may teach a queen.

BACON

You talk treason and death.
The old order is dead, and you and your house will die
With it if you cannot learn.

ESSEX

So said King John
Under the oak, or wherever he was standing,
And little he got by it, as you may recall.
What the devil's a king but a man, or a queen but a
   woman ?

BACON

King John is dead; this is Elizabeth,
Queen in her own right, daughter of a haughty line.
There is one man in all her kingdom she fears
And that man's yourself, and she has good reason to fear
   you.

You're a man not easily governed, a natural rebel,
Moreover, a general, popular and acclaimed,
And, last, she loves you, which makes you the more to be
    feared,
Whether you love her or not.

ESSEX

I do love her !   I do !

BACON

My lord, a man as young as you —

ESSEX

If she were my mother's kitchen hag,
Toothless and wooden-legged, she'd make all others
Colorless.

BACON

You play dangerously there, my lord.

ESSEX

I've never yet loved or hated
For policy nor a purpose.   I tell you she's a witch —
And has a witch's brain.   I love her, I fear her,
I hate her, I adore her —

BACON

That side of it you must know
For yourself.

ESSEX

I will walk softly — here is my hand.
Distress yourself no more — I can carry myself.

BACON

Only count not too much on the loves of queens.

ESSEX

I'll remember.
[CECIL *and* RALEIGH *reappear in the doorway at the right.* RALEIGH *is wearing ordinary armor and carries his silver suit.* ESSEX *looks at him, biting his lip.*]
Sir Walter, take care of your health !

RALEIGH

My health, sir ?

ESSEX

[*Going out.*]
Wearing no silver, in this chilly weather.

RALEIGH

[*Tossing his silver armor into the pile*] Put that with the others.

FIRST GUARD

Are we to wear them, sir ?

RALEIGH

No. Melt them down and sell the silver. And thus see for yourself how soon a fool is parted from his money. Take station in the outer hall and carry this trash with you.

FIRST GUARD

Yes, sir.
[*The guards go out right.*]

RALEIGH

[*To* BACON] And you, sir, you are his friend. . .

BACON

And yours, Sir Walter. . .

RALEIGH

It's the first I've heard of it, but if you're mine too, so much the better.   Carry this news to him: his suits go to the melting-pot.

BACON

Willingly, my lord, if I see him.   You have done quite properly.

RALEIGH

. I do not ask your commendation !

BACON

No, but you have it.
[*He bows low and goes out to left.*]

RALEIGH

There's the viper under our flower, this Francis.
He should be on the winning side.

CECIL

He will be yet . . .
Like all wise men.   For myself, I no longer
Stomach Lord Essex.   Every word he speaks
Makes me feel queasy.

RALEIGH

Then why put up with him ?

CECIL

The queen, my friend, the queen.   What she wants she will have,
And she must have her earl.

RALEIGH

Which does she love more,
Her earl or her kingdom ?

CECIL

Yes, which ?   I have wondered.

RALEIGH

Then you're less sapient
Than I've always thought you, Cecil.   She loves her
    kingdom
More than all men, and always will.   If he could
Be made to look like a rebel, which he's close to be-
    ing . . .
And she could be made to believe it, which is harder,
You'd be first man in the council.

CECIL

And you would be ? . . .

RALEIGH

Wherever I turn he's stood
Square in my way !   My life long here at court
He's snatched honor and favor from before my eyes . . .
Till his voice and walk and aspect make me writhe . . .
There's a fatality in it !

CECIL

If he could be sent from England . . . we might have a
    chance
To come between them.

RALEIGH

Would she let him go ?

CECIL

No . . . but if he could be teased
And stung about his generalship till he was
Too angry to reflect. . . Suppose you were proposed
As general for the next Spanish raid ?

RALEIGH

He would see it,
And so would she.

CECIL

Then if you were named
For the expedition to Ireland ?

RALEIGH

No, I thank you.
He'd let me go, and I'd be sunk in a bog
This next three hundred years.   I've seen enough
Good men try to conquer Ireland.

CECIL

Then how would this be ?
We name three men for Ireland of his own supporters;
He will oppose them, not wishing his party weakened
At the court.   Then we ask what he suggests
And hint at his name for leader. . .

RALEIGH

Good so far.

CECIL

He will be angry and hint at your name; you will offer
To go if he will.

RALEIGH

No.   Not to Ireland.

Yes !
Do you think he'd let you go with him and share
The military glory ?   It will go hard,
Having once brought up his name, if we do not manage
To ship him alone to Dublin.

We can try it, then,
Always remembering that no matter what
Is said . . . no matter what I say or you . . .
I do not go.   You must get me out of that,
By Christ, for I know Ireland.

I will.   Be easy.

When is the council ?

At nine.

You'll make these suggestions ?

If you'll play up to them.

Count on me. I must look after
These silver soldiers.

At nine then.

Count on me.
[*They go out in opposite directions.*]

CURTAIN

ACT ONE

SCENE II

SCENE: *The queen's study, which adjoins her bed-chambers and the council hall. It is a severe little room, with chairs, a desk and a few books, huge and leather-bound.* PENELOPE *comes in from the bed-chamber and looks out through a curtain opposite. She returns to the chamber, then re-enters to wait.* ESSEX *enters.*

PENELOPE

[*Rising*] Good-morrow, my lord.

ESSEX

Good-morrow, Penelope.   Have I kept the queen ?

PENELOPE

If so, would I acknowledge it ?

ESSEX

I commend me to your discretion.

PENELOPE

Only to my discretion ?

ESSEX

Take her what message you will . . . only let it be
that I am here.

PENELOPE

May I have one moment, my lord ? She is not quite ready.

ESSEX

As many as you like. What is it, my dear ?

PENELOPE

Do you love the queen ?

ESSEX

Is that a fair question, as between maid and man ?

PENELOPE

An honest question.

ESSEX

Then I will answer honestly. Yes, my dear.

PENELOPE

Dearly ?

ESSEX

Yes.

PENELOPE

I would you loved someone who loved you better.

ESSEX

Meaning . . . whom ?

PENELOPE

Meaning . . . no-one. Myself, perhaps. That's no-one. Or . . . anyone who loved you better.

ESSEX

Does she not love me, sweet ?

PENELOPE

She loves you, loves you not, loves you, loves you not. . .

ESSEX

And why do you tell me this ?

PENELOPE

Because I am afraid.

ESSEX

For me ?

PENELOPE

I have heard her when she thought she was alone, walk up and down her room soundlessly, night long, cursing you . . . cursing you because she must love you and could not help herself . . . swearing to be even with you for this love she scorns to bear you. My lord, you anger her too much.

ESSEX

But is this not common to lovers ?

PENELOPE

No. I have never cursed you. And I have good cause.

ESSEX

But if I were your lover, you would, sweet. So thank God I am not.

PENELOPE

I must go and tell her you are here.
[*She lifts her face to be kissed.*]
Goodbye.

ESSEX

Goodbye, my dear.
[*He kisses her.*]
And thank you.

PENELOPE

Will you beware of her?

ESSEX

Lover, beware your lover, might well be an old maxim.
I will beware.

PENELOPE

For I am afraid.
[*A* MAID-IN-WAITING *appears in the doorway.*]

MAID

Her Majesty is ready.

PENELOPE

I will tell her my lord is here.
[*She runs out hastily.* ELIZABETH *enters, signing im-
periously to the maid, who disappears. There is a moment's silence.*]

ELIZABETH

When we met last it was, as I remember,
Ill-met by moonlight, sir.

ESSEX

Well-met by day,
My queen.

ELIZABETH

I had hardly hoped to see you again,
My lord of Essex, after what was vowed
Forever when you left.

ESSEX

You are unkind
To remind me.

ELIZABETH

I think I also used
The word forever, and meant it as much, at least . . .
Therefore, no apology.   Only my Penelope
Passed me just now in the door with eyes and lips
That looked the softer for kissing.   I'm not sure
But I'm inopportune.

ESSEX

She's a crazy child.

ELIZABETH

A child !   That's for me, too, no doubt !   These children
Have their little ways with each other !

ESSEX

Must we begin
With charges and counter-charges, when you know. . .

ELIZABETH

Do I indeed ? . . .
You have been gone a week, at this Wanstock of
yours . . .
And a week's a long time at court.   You forget that I
Must live and draw breath whether I see you or not . . .
And there are other men and women, oh yes, all fully
Equipped for loving and being loved !   Penelope . . .
You find Penelope charming.   And as for me

There's always Mountjoy . . . or Sir Walter . . . the
  handsome,
Sir Walter, the silver-plated . . .

ESSEX

He'll wear no more
Silver at your door.

ELIZABETH

What have you done . . . come, tell me.
I knew this silver would draw fire.   What happened ?

ESSEX

Nothing . . . but the fashion's gone out.

ELIZABETH

No, but tell me !

ESSEX

He happened to be in the way
When the upstairs pot was emptied.
He's gone to change his clothes.

ELIZABETH

You shall not be allowed
To do this to him. . .

ESSEX

[*Moving toward her*]
You shall not be allowed
To mock me, my queen.
[*He kisses her.*]

ELIZABETH

Isn't it strange how one man's kiss can grow
To be like any other's . . . or a woman's
To be like any woman's ?

ESSEX

Not yours for me,
No, and not mine for you, you lying villain,
You villain and queen, you double-tongued seductress,
You bitch of brass !

ELIZABETH

Silver, my dear.   Let me be
A bitch of silver.   It reminds me of Raleigh.

ESSEX

Damn you !

ELIZABETH

Damn you and double-damn you for a damner !
Come some day when I'm in the mood.   What day's
   this ? . . .
Thursday ?   Try   next   Wednesday . . . or   any
   Wednesday
Later on in the summer . . . Any summer
Will do.   Why are you still here ?

ESSEX

Oh, God, if I could but walk out that door
And stay away !

ELIZABETH

It's not locked.

ESSEX

But I'd come back !
Where do you think I've been this last week ?   Trying,
Trying not to be here !   But you see, I am here.

ELIZABETH

Yes, I see.

ESSEX

Why did you plague me without a word ?

ELIZABETH

Why did you not come ?

ESSEX

You are a queen, my queen.   You had proscribed me,
Sent formal word I'd not be admitted if I came.

ELIZABETH

I may have meant it at the time.

ESSEX

I think I have a demon, and you are it !

ELIZABETH

If ever a mocking devil tortured a woman
You're my devil and torture me ! Let us part and
    quickly,
Or there'll be worse to come.   Go.

ESSEX

I tell you I will not.

ELIZABETH

Come to me, my Essex.   Let us be kind
For a moment.   I will be kind.   You need not be.
You are young and strangely winning and strangely
    sweet.
My heart goes out to you wherever you are.
And something in me has drawn you.   But this same
    thing
That draws us together hurts and blinds us until
We strike at one another.   This has gone on

A long while.   It grows worse with the years.   It will
end badly.
Go, my dear, and do not see me again.

ESSEX

All this
Is what I said when last I went away.
Yet here I am.

ELIZABETH

Love someone else, my dear.
I will forgive you.

ESSEX

You mean you would try to forgive me.

ELIZABETH

Aye, but I would.

ESSEX

What would you have to forgive ?
I have tried to love others.   It's empty as ashes.

ELIZABETH

What others ?

ESSEX

No one.

ELIZABETH

What others ?

ESSEX

Everyone.

ELIZABETH

Everyone ?

ESSEX

That too has been your triumph !   What is a cry
Of love in the night, when I am sick and angry

And care not ? I would rather hear your mocking
    laughter —
Your laughter — mocking at me — defying me
Ever to be happy — with another.

ELIZABETH

You have done this to me ?

ESSEX

You have done this to me ! You've made it all empty
Away from you ! And with you too !

ELIZABETH

And me — what of me while you were gone ?

ESSEX

If we
Must quarrel when we meet, why then, for God's sake,
Let us quarrel. At least we can quarrel together.

ELIZABETH

I think if we are to love we must love and be silent —
For when we speak —

ESSEX

I'll be silent then.
And you shall speak —

ELIZABETH

[*Her finger to her lips.*]
Hush !

ESSEX

If you would sometimes heed me —

ELIZABETH

Hush !

ESSEX

Only sometimes — only when I'm right.   If you would
Say to yourself that even your lover might be
Right sometimes, instead of flying instantly
Into opposition as soon as I propose
A shift in policy !

ELIZABETH

But you were wrong !   You were wrong !
A campaign into Spain's pure madness, and to strike at
   Flanders
At the same moment . . . think of the drain in men
And the drain on the treasury, and the risks we'd run
Of being unable to follow success or failure
For lack of troops and money . . . !

ESSEX

[*Letting his arms fall*]
But why lack money . . .
And why lack men ?   There's no richer country in
   Europe
In men or money than England !   It's this same ancient
Unprofitable niggardliness that pinches pennies
And wastes a world of treasure !   You could have all
   Spain,
And Spain's dominions in the new world, an empire
Of untold wealth . . . and you forgo them because
You fear to lay new taxes !

ELIZABETH

I have tried that . . .
And never yet has a warlike expedition
Brought me back what it cost !

You've tried half-measures . . .
Raids on the Spanish coast, a few horsemen sent
Into Flanders and out again, always defeating
Yourself by trying too little !   What I plead for
Is to be bold once, just once, give the gods a chance
To be kind to us . . . walk through this cobweb Philip
And take his lazy cities with a storm
Of troops and ships !
If we are to trifle we might better sit
At home forever, and rot !

Here we sit then,
And rot, as you put it.

I'm sorry. . .

It seems to me
We rot to some purpose here.   I have kept the peace
And kept my people happy and prosperous.

And at what a price . . .
What a cowardly price !

I am no coward, either.
It requires more courage not to fight than to fight
When one is surrounded by hasty hot-heads, urging
Campaigns in all directions.

Think of the name

You will leave. . . They will set you down in histories
As the weasel queen who fought and ran away,
Who struck one stroke, preferably in the back,
And then turned and ran. . .

ELIZABETH

Is it my fame you think of,
Or your own, my lord ?   Have you not built your name
High enough ?   I gave you your chance at Cadiz,
And you took it, and now there's no name in all England
Like yours to the common people.   When we ride in
   the streets
Together, it's Essex they cheer and not their queen.
What more would you have ?

ESSEX

Is it for fear of me
And this hollow cheering you hold me back from Spain ?

ELIZABETH

It's because I believe in peace, and have no faith
In wars or what wars win.

ESSEX

You do not fear me ?

ELIZABETH

Yes, and I fear you, too !   You believe yourself
Fitter to be king than I to be queen !   You are flattered
By this crying of your name by fools !   You trust me no
   more
Than you'd trust . . . Penelope . . . or any other
   woman
To be in power !   You believe you'd rule England better
Because you're a man !

ESSEX

That last is true.   I would.
And that doesn't mean I don't love you . . . remember
    that.
I love you, my queen, madly, beyond all measure,
But that's not to say I cannot see where you fail
As sovereign here, and see that why you fail
When you do is merely because a woman cannot
Act and think like a man.

ELIZABETH

Act and think like a man . . . !
Why should I
Think like a man when a woman's thinking's wiser ?
What do you plan ?   To depose me, take over the
    kingdom ?

ESSEX

[*Smiling*]
You are a touchy queen.

ELIZABETH

I had bad bringing up.
I was never sure who my mother was going to be
Next day, and it shook my nerves.

ESSEX

You're your father's daughter,
I'll swear to that.   I can tell by your inconstancy.

ELIZABETH

I wish you had need
To fear for me . . . or at any rate that I'd never
Let you see how much I'm yours.

ESSEX

But why ?

ELIZABETH

Tell me, my dear,
Do you tire of me . . . do I wear upon you a little ?

ESSEX

Never.

ELIZABETH

But you'd have to say that, you can see . . .
You'd have to say it, because you wouldn't hurt me,
And because I'm your queen.   And so I'll never know
Until everyone else has known and is laughing at me,
When I've lost you.   Wait, let me say this, please . . .
   When the time
Does come, and I seem old to you, and you love
Someone else, tell me, tell me the first . . .

ESSEX

You are not old !   I will not have you old !

ELIZABETH

Will you do that, in all kindness, in memory
Of great love past ?   No.   You could not, could not.
It's not in a man to be kind that way, nor in
A woman to take it kindly.   I think I'd kill you,
In a first blind rage.

ESSEX

Kill me when I can say it.

ELIZABETH

Love, will you let me
Say one more thing that will hurt you ?

Anything.

Your blood's on fire to lead a new command
Now that you've won so handsomely in Spain,
And when I need a general anywhere
You'll ask to go.   Don't ask it . . . and don't go.
You're better here in London.

Was this all you wanted ?
[*Stepping back*]
To make me promise this ?

[*Softly*]
Not for myself,
I swear it, not because I think you reckless
With men and money, though I do think that,
Not because you might return in too much triumph
And take my kingdom from me, which I can imagine,
And not because I want to keep you here
And hate to risk you, though that's also true . . .
But rather . . . and for this you must forgive me . . .
Because you're more a poet than general . . .
And I fear you might fail, and lose what you have gained,
If you went again.

God's death !   Whom would you send ?

I asked you not to be angry.

ESSEX

Not to be angry !
How do you judge a leader except by whether
He wins or loses ?   Was it by chance, do you think,
That I took Cadiz ?

ELIZABETH

Very well.   You shall go.
Go if you will.   Only I love you, and I say
What would be wiser.

ESSEX

You choose the one thing I must have
And ask me not to ask it !   No.   Forgive me.

ELIZABETH

I'll not say it again.

ESSEX

But if I'm more poet than
General, why poets make better generals
Than generals do, on occasion.

ELIZABETH

You've proved it so
On more than one occasion.
[*A clock strikes.   She rises.*]
There's the chime.
The council's waiting, and we shall hear about Ireland,
If Cecil has his way.   One thing remember,
You must not go to Ireland.

ESSEX

No.   That's a war
I'm content to miss.

ELIZABETH

Thank God for that much then.   I've been afraid
Ireland might tempt you.   And one more thing remem-
   ber . . .
I'll have to oppose you in the council on
The Spanish hostages. . . You'll have your way . . .
But I'll have to oppose you, lest they think it's your
   kingdom. . .
Will you understand . . . ?

ESSEX

I'll play my part perfectly.
[*He kisses her hand, then her lips.*]

ELIZABETH

Now what can come between us, out of heaven or hell,
Or Spain or England ?

ESSEX

Nothing . . . never again.

CURTAIN

ACT ONE

SCENE III

SCENE: *The same as Scene I, save that the doors to the council room have been thrown back, revealing a chair of state for the queen, and beneath it a table at which her councillors sit. The* GUARDS *are placed at left and right. The* QUEEN *sits in her chair.* RALEIGH, CECIL, ESSEX, BURGHLEY, HOWARD, *and one or two others are at the table. The queen's* JESTER *sits cross-legged on a mat.* BURGHLEY *is speaking.*

BURGHLEY

It is quite true we shall have an enemy
In Spain while Philip lives and his state has power
To wage war on us, but there is little he can do
Against an island as well walled as ours.
He has tried his best, and failed.   My lord of Essex
Says it costs more to fight Spain every year
In this chronic fashion than it would to throw
A challenge down, raid the Escurial
And sack the empire.   With this the weight of the
    council
Disagrees, and we may hold it settled
That our tactics continue defensive till the queen
Rule otherwise.

44

ELIZABETH

You'll wait some time for that.

BURGHLEY

But in the matter
Of the Spanish ransoms it appears to me
Lord Essex has right on his side. The English soldiers
Who brought their prisoners home from the last raid
Deserve their prize money. By immemorial custom
The ransom belongs to the taker of the prisoner
And not to the state.

ELIZABETH

That I intend to change,
That same immemorial custom. I thought you had
    been
Informed, Lord Burghley, that it was my will
That the Spanish ransoms be paid to the treasury.

BURGHLEY

But my lord of Essex . . .

ELIZABETH

My lord of Essex does not speak for me.
I was told this expedition into Spain
Would be paid for in booty. The cost, so far,
Has not been made up; and since there are Spanish
    nobles
To be ransomed, I think they should pay it.

ESSEX

Your Majesty,
I do not speak for myself . . . I took no prizes . . .

But only to redeem my word.   I assured
My followers that they would have for their own
Whatever ransoms they earned.

ELIZABETH

And by what right
Did you make this promise?

ESSEX

By this same ancient custom
Of which Lord Burghley speaks.   A custom so well
Established there's not a soldier anywhere
But takes it for granted.

ELIZABETH

Your word is pledged?

ESSEX

It is.

ELIZABETH

[*Smiling*]
And if the state should confiscate these ransoms
You would make them good to the captors?

ESSEX

No.   To speak frankly . . .
[*He smiles*]
No.

ELIZABETH

Then the issue lies between the queen
And her soldiers . . . and your lordship need feel no
Concern in the matter.

ESSEX

When I made these promises
I spoke for Your Majesty . . . or believed I did.

ELIZABETH

Master Cecil, advise us; am I as queen
Bound by Lord Essex' promise ?

CECIL

No, my liege;
It is well-known a regent may repudiate
Treaty or word of a subject officer.
The throne is not bound.

ESSEX

If it comes to repudiation,
The throne can, of course, repudiate what it likes.
But not without breaking faith.

ELIZABETH

I fear we are wrong, Sir Robert;
And what has been promised for me and in my name
By my own officer, my delegate in the field,
I must perform.   The men may have their ransoms.
The state will take its loss; for this one time
Only, and this the last.   In the future a prisoner
Is held in the name of the state, and whatever price
Is on his head belongs to the crown.   Our action
Here is made no precedent.   What further
Business is there before us ?

CECIL

There is one perpetual
Subject, Your Majesty, which we take up

Time after time, and always leave unsettled,
But which has come to a place where we must act
One way or another.   Tyrone's rebellion in Ulster
Is no longer a smouldering coal, but a running fire
Spreading north to south.   We must conquer Ireland
Finally now, or give over what we have won.
Ireland's not Spain.

ELIZABETH

I grant you.

THE FOOL

I also grant you.

ELIZABETH

Be quiet, fool.

THE FOOL

Be quiet, fool.
[*He slaps his own mouth.*]

ELIZABETH

Lord Burghley,
You shall speak first.   What's to be done in Ireland?

BURGHLEY

If my son is right, and I believe him to be,
We can bide our time no longer there.   They have
Some help from Spain, and will have more, no doubt,
And the central provinces are rising.   We must
Stamp out this fire or lose the island.

ELIZABETH

This means
Men, money, ships?

BURGHLEY

Yes, madam.

CECIL

And more than that . . .
A leader.

ELIZABETH

What leader ?

CECIL

A Lord Protector
Of Ireland who can carry sword and fire
From one end of the bogs to the other, and have English
   law
On Irish rebels till there are no rebels.
We've governed Ireland with our left hand, so far,
And our hold is slipping.   The man who goes there now
Must be one fitted to master any field . . .
The best we have.

ELIZABETH

What man ?   Name one.

CECIL

We should send,
Unless I am wrong, a proved and able general,
Of no less rank, say, than Lord Howard here,
Lord Essex, Sir Walter Raleigh, Knollys, or Mount-
   joy . . .
This is no slight matter, to keep or lose the island.

ELIZABETH

I grant you that also.

THE FOOL

I also grant you.   Be quiet,
Fool !
[*He slaps his mouth.*]

ELIZABETH

I ask you for one and you name a dozen,
Sir Robert.

RALEIGH

Why should one go alone, if it comes
To that ?   Why not two expeditions, one
To Dublin, one into Ulster, meeting half-way ?

ELIZABETH

Are there two who could work together ?

CECIL

Knollys and Mountjoy.
They are friends and of one house.

ESSEX

Yes, of my house.

ELIZABETH

Essex, whom would you name ?

ESSEX

Why, since Lord Cecil
Feels free to name my followers, I shall feel free
To name one or two of his. . .

ELIZABETH

In other words,
You would rather Knollys and Mountjoy did not go ?

ESSEX

I would rather they stayed in England, as Sir Robert
knows.
I have need of them here. But I will spare one of
them
If Lord Cecil will let Sir Francis Vere go with him.

ELIZABETH

Let Vere and Knollys go.

CECIL

Lord Essex names
Sir Francis Vere because he knows full well
I cannot spare him, my liege.

ELIZABETH

Is this appointment
To wait for all our private bickerings?
Can we send no man of worth to Ireland, merely
Because to do so would weaken some house or party
Here at court?

THE FOOL

Your Majesty has said . . .

ELIZABETH

Be quiet. . .

THE FOOL

Fool!

ELIZABETH

Be quiet!

THE FOOL

Fool!

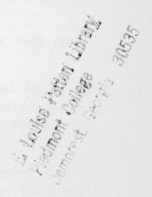

ELIZABETH

Be quiet !
[*The* FOOL *forms the word "fool" with his lips, but
makes no sound.*]

CECIL

[*Rising*]
I hope I betray no secret, Sir Walter,
If I tell the council that I spoke with you
Before the session, and asked you if you would go
Into Ireland if the queen requested it . . . and that
    you said
Yes, should the queen desire it.

BURGHLEY

That would answer.

CECIL

But I believe, and Sir Walter believes, there should be
More than one hand in this . . . that if he goes
Lord Essex should go with him.

ELIZABETH

With him ?

ESSEX

In what
Capacity ?

CECIL

Leading an equal command. Two generals
Of coeval power, landing north and south
And meeting to crush Tyrone.

ESSEX

Would you set up
Two Lord Protectors ?

CECIL

It was my thought that we name
Raleigh as Lord Protector.

ESSEX

And I under him ?

CECIL

Since the Azores adventure
Which my Lord Essex led, and which came off
A little lamer than could be wished, but in which
Sir Walter showed to very great advantage,
It has seemed to me that Raleigh should receive
First place if he served in this.

ESSEX

[*Rising*]
This is deliberate,
An insult planned !

CECIL

It is no insult, my lord,
But plain truth.   I speak for the good of the state.

ESSEX

You lie !   You have never spoken here or elsewhere
For any cause but your own !

ELIZABETH

No more of this !

ESSEX

The good of the state ! Good God !
Am I to swallow this from a clerk, a pen-pusher . . .
To be told I may have second place, for the good of
the state ?

CECIL

Were you not wrong at the Azores ?

ESSEX

No, by God !
And you know it !

ELIZABETH

Whoever makes you angry has won
Already, Essex !

ESSEX

They have planned this !

CECIL

I say no more.
Raleigh will go to Ireland as Lord Protector
And go alone, if the queen asks it of him,
And since you will not go.

ESSEX

I have not said
I would not go. But if I were to go I would go
Alone, as Lord Protector !

ELIZABETH

That you will not.
I have some word in this.

If this pet rat
Lord Cecil wishes to know my mind about him,
And it seems he does, he shall have it ! How he first crept
Into favor here I know not, but the palace is riddled
With his spying and burrowing and crawling under-
     ground !
He has filled the court with his rat friends, very gentle,
White, squeaking, courteous folk, who show their teeth
Only when cornered; who smile at you, speak you fair
And spend their nights gnawing the floors and chairs
Out from under us all !

My lord !

I am
Not the gnawing kind, nor will I speak fair
To those who don't mean me well . . . no, nor to those
To whom I mean no good ! I say frankly here,
Yes, to their faces, that Cecil and Walter Raleigh
Have made themselves my enemies because
They cannot brook greatness or power in any but
Themselves ! And I say this to them . . . and to the
     world. . .
I, too, have been ambitious, as all men are
Who bear a noble mind, but if I rise
It will be by my own effort, and not by dragging
Better men down through intrigue ! I admit
Sir Walter Raleigh's skill as a general
And Cecil's statecraft ! I could work with them freely

And cheerfully, but every time I turn
My back they draw their knives! When Cecil left
    England
I guarded his interests as I would my own
Because he asked me to . . . but when I left,
And left my affairs in his hands . . . on my return
I found my plans and my friends out in the rain
Along with the London beggars!

CECIL

I did my best. . .

ESSEX

Aye . . . the best for yourself! For the good of the
    state !

RALEIGH

If Lord Essex wishes
To say he is my enemy, very well . . .
He is my enemy.

ESSEX

But you were mine first. . .
And I call the gods to witness you would be my friend
Still, if I'd had my way! I take it hard
That here, in the queen's council, where there should be
Magnanimous minds if anywhere, there is still
No trust or friendship!

ELIZABETH

I take it hard that you
Should quarrel before me.

ESSEX

Would you have us quarrel
Behind your back ?   It suits them all too well
To quarrel in secret and knife men down in the dark !

BURGHLEY

This is fantastic, my lord.   There has been no knifing.
Let us come to a decision.   We were discussing
The Irish protectorate.

CECIL

And as for Ireland,
I am willing to leave that in Lord Essex' hands
To do as he decides.

ESSEX

Send your Sir Walter
To Ireland as Protector !   And be damned to it !

CECIL

As the queen wishes.
It is a task both difficult and dangerous.
I cannot blame Lord Essex for refusing
To risk his fame there.

ESSEX

There speaks the white rat again !
Yet even a rat should know I have never refused
A task out of fear !   I said I would not go
As second in command !

CECIL

Then would you go
As Lord Protector ?

ELIZABETH

You have named your man . . .
Sir Walter Raleigh.

RALEIGH

I'll go if Essex goes.

ESSEX

What ! Is our Raleigh
Afraid to go alone ?

RALEIGH

I don't care for it . . .
And neither does our Essex !

ESSEX

Why, what is this
That hangs over Ireland ? Is it haunted, this Ireland ?
Is it a kind of hell where men are damned
If they set foot on it ? I've never seen the place,
But if it's a country like other countries, with people
Like other people in it, it's nothing to be
Afraid of, more than France or Wales or Flanders
Or anywhere else !

CECIL

We hear you say so.

ESSEX

If I
Am challenged to go to Ireland, then, Christ, I'll go !
Give me what men and horse I need, and put me
In absolute charge, and if I fail to bring

This Tyrone's head back with me, and put the rebellion
To sleep forever, take my sword from me
And break it . . . I'll never use it again !

ELIZABETH

Will you listen . . . ?

ESSEX

They've challenged me !

ELIZABETH

If you volunteer
To go to Ireland there is none to stop you.
You are first soldier here, first in acclaim
And in achievement, but since the decision lies
With yourself alone, reflect a little.

ESSEX

My queen,
I can see that Raleigh and Cecil have set themselves
To bait me into Ireland !   They know and I know
That Ireland has been deadly to any captain
Who risked his fortunes there; moreover, once
I'm gone they think to strip me here at home,
Ruin me both ways !   And I say to them "Try it !"
There are men who are greater than Ireland or their
   chicane. . .
Since this is a challenge I go, and go alone,
And return victorious, and, by God, more of a problem
To Cecils and Raleighs than when I went !
[*The* FOOL *rises and approaches* ESSEX *from behind.*]

BURGHLEY

If Essex
Will go, it solves our problem, Your Majesty.
We could hardly refuse that offer.

ELIZABETH

No.

ESSEX

I will go,
And I will return !   Mark me !

THE FOOL

[*Touching* ESSEX]
My lord !   My lord !

ESSEX

[*Turning suddenly with an instinctive motion that
sweeps the* FOOL *to the floor.*]
Take your hands off me !   You touch me for a fool ?
[*He helps the* FOOL *up.*]
Get up !

THE FOOL

Do not go to Ireland !

ESSEX

[*Impatiently*]
You too ?

THE FOOL

Because, my lord, I come from Ireland.
All the best fools come from Ireland, but only
A very great fool will go there.

ESSEX

Faugh !

THE FOOL

It's not too late yet !

ELIZABETH

Break up the council, my lords.
We meet tomorrow.

BURGHLEY

And this is decided ?

ESSEX

Yes !

ELIZABETH

Yes, if you wish it.   Go now.
[*The council rises when the queen does and files out
silently, leaving* Essex *and* ELIZABETH.]
You should have had
The fool's brain and he yours !   You would have bet-
   tered
By the exchange.

ESSEX

I thank you kindly, lady.

ELIZABETH

What malicious star
Danced in my sky when you were born, I wonder ?

ESSEX

What malicious star danced in the sky
Of Ireland, you should ask.

ELIZABETH

Oh, my dear,
You are a child in council.   I saw them start
To draw you into this, and tried to warn you . . .
But it was no use.

ESSEX

They drew me into nothing.
I saw their purpose and topped it with my own.
Let them believe they've sunk me.

ELIZABETH

You will withdraw.
I'll countermand this.

ESSEX

And give them the laugh on me ?
I'll have the laugh on them yet.

ELIZABETH

Better they should laugh
A little now than laugh at you forever.

ESSEX

And why not win in Ireland ?

ELIZABETH

No man wins there.
You're so dazzled
With the chance to lead an army you'd follow the devil
In an assault on heaven.

ESSEX

No, but I'd lead him.
Heaven is always taken by storm.   That's one thing

The devil doesn't know. Ireland is only
A country, and this is superstition.

ELIZABETH

I know.
You were quite right. I thought so as you said it.
Only somehow here in my breast something con-
    stricts . . .
Is it the heart grows heavy ? I must let you go . . .
And I'll never see you again.

ESSEX

Mistrust all these
Forebodings. When they prove correct we remember
    them,
But when they're wrong we forget them. They mean
    nothing.
Remember this when I'm back and all turns out
    well . . .
That you felt all would turn out badly.

ELIZABETH

Oh, my love,
Come touch me, tell me all will happen well.

ESSEX

And so it will.

ELIZABETH

Do you want to go ?

ESSEX

Why yes . . .
And no. I've said I would and I will.

ELIZABETH

It's not yet
Too late.   There are no announcements made, no orders
Given.   If you win, that will divide us . . .
And if you lose, that will divide us too.

ESSEX

I'll win, and it will not divide us.   Is it so hard
To believe in me ?

ELIZABETH

No . . . I'll believe in you . . .
And even forgive you if you need it.   Here.
My father gave me this ring . . . and told me if ever
He lost his temper with me, to bring it to him
And he'd forgive me.   And so it saved my life . . .
Long after, when he'd forgotten, long after, when
One time he was angry.

ESSEX

Darling, if ever
You're angry rings won't help.

ELIZABETH

Yes, but it would.
I'd think of you as you are now, and it would.
Take it.

ESSEX

I have no pledge from you.   I'll take it
To remember you in absence.

ELIZABETH

Take it for a better reason.   Take it because
The years are long, and full of sharp, wearing days

That wear out what we are and what we have been
And change us into people we do not know,
Living among strangers. Lest you and I who love
Should wake some morning strangers and enemies
In an alien world, far off; take my ring, my lover.

ESSEX

You fear
You will not always love me?

ELIZABETH

No, that you
Will not love me, and will not let me love you.
[*She puts the ring on his finger.*]

CURTAIN

ACT TWO

SCENE I

SCENE: *The queen's study.* PENELOPE *is sitting read-ing. The* FOOL *enters. She does not see him.*

THE FOOL

Sh ! Make no noise.

PENELOPE

What do you mean ?

THE FOOL

Silence ! Quiet !

PENELOPE

I am silent, fool.

THE FOOL

You silent ? And even as you say it you are talking !

PENELOPE

You began it.

THE FOOL

Began what ?

PENELOPE

Talking.

66

THE FOOL

Oh, no.   Talking began long before my time.   It was a woman began it.

PENELOPE

Her name ?

THE FOOL

Penelope, I should judge.

PENELOPE

Fool.

THE FOOL

[*Looking away*] No, for with this same Penelope began also beauty and courage and tenderness and faith . . . all that a man could desire or a woman offer . . . and all that this early Penelope began has a later Penelope completed.

PENELOPE

[*Rising*]   It lacked only this . . . that the court fool should make love to me.

THE FOOL

I am sorry to have been laggard.   But truly I have never found you alone before.

PENELOPE

How lucky I've been !

THE FOOL

Are you angered ?

PENELOPE

At what ?

THE FOOL

At my loving you.

PENELOPE

I've learned to bear nearly everything.

THE FOOL

A lover's absence ?

PENELOPE

Among other things.

THE FOOL

The presence of suitors undesired ?

PENELOPE

That, too.

THE FOOL

I am not a suitor, my lady. I ask nothing. I know
where your heart lies. It is with my lord Essex in Ireland. I do not love you.

PENELOPE

Good.

THE FOOL

I lied to you. I do love you.

PENELOPE

I am sorry.

THE FOOL

You will not laugh at me ?

PENELOPE

No.

THE FOOL

Then there is yet some divinity in the world . . . while a woman can still be sorry for one who loves her without return.

PENELOPE

A woman is sadly aware that when a man loves her it makes a fool of him.

THE FOOL

And if a fool should love a woman . . . would it not make a man of him?

PENELOPE

No, but doubly a fool, I fear.

THE FOOL

And the women . . . how of the women?

PENELOPE

They have been fools, too.

THE FOOL

The more fool I, I tried to save Lord Essex from Ireland . . . but he needs must go . . . the more fool he.

PENELOPE

Let us not talk of that.

THE FOOL

May I kiss you?

PENELOPE

No.

THE FOOL

Your hand?

PENELOPE

Yes.
[*He kisses her hand.*]

THE FOOL

I thank you.
[*She touches his fool's cap gently with her hand.*]

PENELOPE

The more fool you, poor boy.
[ROBERT CECIL *enters from the left.*]

CECIL

This is hardly a seemly pastime, Mistress Gray.

PENELOPE

And are you now the judge of what is seemly, Sir Robert ?

CECIL

[*To the* FOOL] Be off with you !   [*To* PENELOPE] The queen is expecting Master Bacon here ?
[*The* FOOL *goes.*]

PENELOPE

I am set to wait for him.

CECIL

You will not be needed.

PENELOPE

Excellent.   [*She goes out right, passing* RALEIGH, *who enters.*]

CECIL

This Bacon keeps himself close. I have been unable to speak with him. She has this news?

RALEIGH

Yes.

CECIL

She believes it?

RALEIGH

Burghley himself believes it.

CECIL

Then she does.

RALEIGH

Beyond question.
[*The curtains part at the left and* BACON *enters.*]

CECIL

Good-morrow, Master Bacon.

BACON

And to you, my lords.

CECIL

I have sent everywhere for you, sir, this three hours . . . and perhaps it was not altogether by accident that I could not find you.

BACON

I was not at home. You must forgive me.

CECIL

You are here to see the queen?

BACON

[*Bowing*] The queen has also been good enough to send for me.

CECIL

It was my wish to speak with you first . . . and it is my opinion that it will be the better for all of us, if I do so now . . . late as it is.

BACON

I am but barely on time, gentlemen.

CECIL

You need answer one question only. You have been in correspondence with Lord Essex in Ireland ?

BACON

Perhaps.

CECIL

The queen has this morning received news warning her that Lord Essex is allied with the Irish rebels and is even now leading his army back to England to usurp her throne. Had you heard this ?

BACON

No.

CECIL

Do you credit it ?

BACON

It is your own scheme, I believe.

CECIL

That Essex should rebel against the queen ?

BACON

Even so.

RALEIGH

You accuse us of treason?

BACON

If the queen were aware of certain matters she would herself accuse you of treason.

CECIL

What matters?

BACON

I prefer that the queen should question me.

CECIL

Look to yourself, Master Bacon. If you intend to accuse any man of the suppression of letters written by Essex to the queen, or of the suppression of letters sent by the queen to Essex, you will be unable to prove these assertions and you will argue yourself very neatly into the Tower.

BACON

My lord . . . I had no such business in mind.

RALEIGH

Then what? . . .

BACON

I hope I can keep my own counsel. The truth is, my lords, you are desperate men. You have overreached yourselves, and if wind of it gets to the royal ears you are done.

RALEIGH

We shall drag a few down with us if we are done, though, and you the first.

CECIL

You have but a poor estimate of me, Master Bacon. If you go in to the queen and reveal to her that her letters to Essex have not reached him . . . as you mean to do . . . the queen will then send for me, and I will send for Lord Essex' last letter to you, containing a plan for the capture of the city of London. It will interest you to know that I have read that letter and you are learned enough in the law to realize in what light you will stand as a witness should the queen see it.

BACON

I think it is true, though, that if I go down I shall also drag a few with me, including those here present.

CECIL

I am not so sure of that, either. I am not unready for that contingency. But to be frank with you, it would be easier for both you and us if you were on our side.

BACON

You must expect a man to side with his friends.

CECIL

And a man's friends . . . who are they ? Those who can help him to what he wants.

BACON

Not always.

CECIL

When he is wise.   You have served Lord Essex well and
I believe he has made you promises.   But the moment
Essex enters England in rebellion, he is doomed, and
his friends with him.

BACON

One word from the queen to him . . . one word from
him to the queen . . . one word from me, revealing
that their letters have been intercepted, and there can be
no talk of rebellion.   There has been some underhand
traffic with the couriers between here and Ireland. Their
letters have been lost, you have induced the queen to
promulgate arbitrary orders . . . and since they are
both proud, you have bred distrust in her and defiance
in him.   Your machinations have been so direct, so
childish, so simple . . . and so simply exposed . . .
that I wonder at you !

CECIL

My friend, a child could trip him.   Not so simple as
your own.   I have news this morning that Lord Essex
has already landed in England and set up his standard
here.   He is a rebel, and when a man is once a rebel,
do you think there will be any careful inquiry into how
he happened to become one ?

BACON

Essex in England !

CECIL

In England.

RALEIGH

And has neglected to disband his army.

CECIL

You speak of explanations between the queen and Essex.
Unless you betray us there will be no explanations.
They are at war and will never meet again.

BACON

That is, if your plan succeed.

CECIL

[*Standing aside*] Very well, then. Go in. You have
chosen your master. I have done with you.

BACON

[*Not moving*] And if I say nothing ?

CECIL

Then . . . whatever you have been promised, whatever
you have desired, that you shall have. There is no place
in the courts you could not fill. You shall have your
choice. If you need excuse, no-one should know better
than you that this Essex is a danger to the state, a danger
to the queen, a danger to liberty.

BACON

If I need excuse I shall find one for myself. [*There is
a pause. Then the curtain parts to the right and* PENEL-
OPE *enters. She holds the curtain back.*]

PENELOPE

Yes, Your Majesty; he is here.

ELIZABETH

Why was I not told ? [*She enters.*] Is this an ante-
chamber, Sir Robert ? Am I never to look out of my
room without seeing you ?

CECIL

Your pardon, Your Majesty. I was just going.

ELIZABETH

Then go. You need not pause to explain why you came. I am weary of your face!

CECIL

Yes, Your Majesty.
[CECIL *and* RALEIGH *bow and depart.*]

ELIZABETH

I have heard that you are a shrewd man, Master Bacon.

BACON

Flattery, Majesty, flattery.

ELIZABETH

I have heard it,
And in a sort I believe it. Tell me one thing . . .
Are you Cecil's friend?

BACON

I have never been.

ELIZABETH

He is a shrewd man; he's
A man to make a friend of if you'd stand well
In the court, sir.

BACON

It may be so.

ELIZABETH

Why are you not
His friend then?

BACON

We are not on the same side.

ELIZABETH

You follow Lord Essex ?

BACON

Since I have known him.

ELIZABETH

There's
A dangerous man to follow.

BACON

Lord Essex ?

ELIZABETH

Lord Essex.

BACON

I am sorry, madam,
If I have displeased you.

ELIZABETH

You have displeased me.

BACON

I repeat then . . .
I am sorry.

ELIZABETH

You will change, then ?   You will forget
This Essex of yours ?

BACON

If you ask it . . . if there is reason . . .

ELIZABETH

Well, there is reason !   He has taken up arms
Against me in Ireland.

BACON

You are sure of this?

ELIZABETH

I have reports.   Is it so hard to believe?

BACON

Without proofs, it is.

ELIZABETH

I have proof.

BACON

May I ask of what sort?

ELIZABETH

Proof good enough.   You know the punishment
For treason?   From what I have heard
Of late both you and Essex should remember
That punishment.

BACON

Madam, for myself I have
No need to fear, and if Lord Essex has
I am more than mistaken in him.

ELIZABETH

I am very sorry
That I must do this . . . but all friends of Essex
Go straightway to the Tower.   I have sent for you
To give you a last chance to change your mind
Before this blow falls.   Are you still his friend?

BACON

Yes, Majesty.

ELIZABETH

I am sorry for it.

BACON

That is all ?

ELIZABETH

Why, no.   You do not believe me ?

BACON

I do not.

ELIZABETH

And why ?

BACON

I neither believe our Essex a rebel
Nor that you believe so.   If you intended to place me
In the Tower . . . I would be in the Tower . . . and
   no talk about it.

ELIZABETH

You are shrewd indeed.

BACON

I am Essex' friend.

ELIZABETH

If that
Were true . . . if I could speak to you . . . if there
   were only
The sound of one honest voice !
. . . I must rule England,
And they say he is rebel to me . . . and day and night,
Waking, sleeping, in council, there is still always
One thing crying out in me over and again . . .

Waking and sleeping I hear it crying: He cannot,
Cannot fail me ! But I have written him my love
And he has not answered. What you know of this
Answer me truly, truly . . . bitter or not,
And you shall not lose !

BACON

He has not answered ?

ELIZABETH

No.

BACON

If I
Knew why I would know much. Have you angered
  him . . .
Sent arbitrary orders ?

ELIZABETH

I have ordered him to disband
His forces and return. I have cut off
Revenue and supplies.

BACON

But this was rash . . .
To send a popular leader out with an army
And then check him suddenly, heap disgrace upon
  him . . .
He has great pride.

ELIZABETH

[Getting up]
He has rebelled then ?
I wrote him lovingly.

BACON

And he answered ? . . .

ELIZABETH

Nothing.

BACON

That could not be excused.

ELIZABETH

And it cannot be. It's true. It will not be !

BACON

Dear queen, I fear
I have turned you against him !

ELIZABETH

No, no ! I needed that !

BACON

And if there were something wrong . . .
Some misunderstanding ? . . .

ELIZABETH

No, no . . . don't try comfort now . . .
He had my letters. That could not go wrong.
Did he not have my letters ?

BACON

Could it be otherwise ?

ELIZABETH

You would know that. You would know if he had
    not.
You've had word from him ?

BACON

Yes.

ELIZABETH

He has written you,
But not me ! Or are you traitor to him also ? . . .
I think you are ! I think you lie to me ! I am
Encompassed by lies ! I think you, too, betray
  him . . .
But subtly, with infinite craft, making me believe
First that you would not wrong him ! No, no . . .
  I'm gone mad
Pacing my room, pacing the room of my mind.
They say a woman's mind is an airless room,
Sunless and airless, where she must walk alone
Saying he loves me, loves me, loves me not,
And has never loved me. The world goes by, all
  shadows,
And there are voices, all echoes till he speaks . . .
And there's no light till his presence makes a light
There in that room. But I am a queen. Where I
  walk
Is a hall of torture, where the curious gods bring all
Their racks and gyves, and stretch me there to writhe
Till I cry out. They watch me with eyes of iron
Waiting to hear what I cry ! I am crying now . . .
Listen, you gods of iron ! He never loved me . . .
He wanted my kingdom only . . .
Loose me and let me go ! I am yet a queen . . .
That I have ! That he will not take from me.
I shall be queen, and walk his room no more.
He thought to break me down by not answering . . .
Break me until I'd say, I'm all yours . . . what I am

And have, all yours ! That I will never, never,
Never say. I'm not broken yet.

BACON

Nor will be, majesty.

ELIZABETH

We must not follow him.
We must forget him, break him as he would break us,
Bow that bright head . . . I shall be as I was.
See him no more, my friend,
He walks on quicksand. Avoid him.

BACON

Yes, my queen.

ELIZABETH

Go, my friend.
You have done well. I trust you.

BACON

I thank Your Majesty.
[*He goes out.* ELIZABETH *claps her hands twice.*
After a moment CAPTAIN ARMIN *enters.*]

ELIZABETH

Captain Armin, keep a watch on Master Bacon,
On his house and on his correspondence.
I wish to know all he knows.

ARMIN

Yes, Your Majesty.

ELIZABETH

Wait. I have found you true of word,

And sure of hand. Moreover, you can keep counsel —
[ARMIN *bows. She beckons him to come to her. He
does so.*]
What we say now is forever secret between us —
Between us two — not one other.

ARMIN

I'll hold it so.

ELIZABETH

It is reported there is an army risen
Against me —

ARMIN

God forbid !

ELIZABETH

It is so reported. The rebellion I speak of's the force
Lord Essex has brought back with him from Ireland.
I wish to make this preparation for it: Whatever orders
You receive from your superiors, whatever broils
Occur, he is to have free access to my presence.

ARMIN

There would be danger to your person, madame.

ELIZABETH

I will risk that.

ARMIN

You would be hostage if he were in command.

ELIZABETH

Be ready for danger — and if need be, death.

ARMIN

Yes, Majesty.
[*He goes out.* ELIZABETH *stands motionless for a*

*moment.   There is a sudden burst of girls' laughter in
an adjoining room, and the* FOOL *runs in with a gar-
ment in his hand.   Three* GIRLS *run after him, the fore-
most tripping him so that he falls in a corner and is
instantly pounced upon by all three.*]

MARY

[*Entering*] Thief !   Thief !   Stop thief !

ELLEN

Kill the slobber thief !   Fall on him !

TRESSA

Can a maid not keep a silk smock ?

THE FOOL

Help !   Salvage !   Men-at-arms to the rescue !   I am
boarded by pirates !
[*They tickle him.*]

ELLEN

Tear it from him !   He will exhibit it !

TRESSA

No, no !   Don't tear it !

THE FOOL

If you sit on me in that fashion, darling, you will regret
it.   There will be issue !

ELLEN

What issue ?

THE FOOL

Twins !   Seven or eight !
[ELLEN *slaps him*.]

MARY

Rise !   Rise quickly !   The queen is here.   Rise !
[*They all get up in confusion*.]

TRESSA

We are sorry, your Majesty.
[ELIZABETH *looks at them without seeing them, and goes out to her bedroom*.]

ELLEN

What is it ?   She seemed not to see.

MARY

It's not like her not to strike us.

TRESSA

We'll be whipped.

THE FOOL

No, no.   She strikes instantly or not at all.

TRESSA

Give me that.   [*She snatches her smock from the* FOOL.]

MARY

Come.
[*They tiptoe out*.]

CURTAIN

ACT TWO

SCENE II

SCENE: *The interior of Essex' tent on the coast of England.* ESSEX *sits in the light of a candle, reading dispatches.* A GUARD *stands in the shadow.* MARVEL, *an aide, enters.*

MARVEL

There is a courier from the queen, my lord.

ESSEX

At last, then.

MARVEL

You will see him at once ?

ESSEX

Yes . . . Wait. Bring him in and stay here while I read the dispatches. If I give orders to torture or kill him, show no surprise. You understand ?

MARVEL

You will not torture him ?

ESSEX

Am I not tortured ? And you, too, sirrah. You will remember ?

THE GUARD

Yes, my lord.

ESSEX

Good.

[MARVEL *goes out.* ESSEX *rises and stands out of the light, waiting.* MARVEL *enters with the* COURIER, *who falls on his knee before* ESSEX.]

THE COURIER

My lord of Essex ?

ESSEX

Yes.

COURIER

Dispatches from the queen.

ESSEX

When did you leave London ?

COURIER

Four days ago, my lord.   We were delayed.

ESSEX

What delayed you ?

COURIER

Robbers.

ESSEX

And they took what from you ?

COURIER

Our horses and money.

ESSEX

And the letters ? . . .

COURIER

Were returned to me untouched.

ESSEX

When did this happen ?

COURIER

This side of the ford. There were four armed men against us two.

ESSEX

Give me the letters.
[*The* COURIER *does so*. ESSEX *reads briefly*.]
This is all ?

COURIER

Yes, my lord.

ESSEX

You are sure you have lost nothing ?

COURIER

Indeed yes, my lord. There was but one missive and the seal was returned unbroken. The cut-throats told us they cared the less about our letters for they could not read.

ESSEX

You are a clever liar, sirrah, and you are the third liar who has come that same road to me from London.

You are the third liar to tell this same tale. You shall pay for being the third.

COURIER

My lord, I have not lied to you.

ESSEX

Take his weapons from him, lieutenant. [MARVEL *obeys*.] Set him against the post there. Not so gently. He shall lose his ears first and then his lying tongue.

COURIER

Your lordship does not mean this?

ESSEX

And why not? We shall then cut him in pieces . . . but gradually, with infinite delicacy.
[MARVEL *approaches the* COURIER *with a knife. The* GUARD *holds him.*]

COURIER

No, no, no, no! Oh, God! Oh, my lord! My lord!

ESSEX

What are you waiting for?

MARVEL

We must tie him to the pole first, sir.

ESSEX

Then tie him!

COURIER

No, no . . . oh, God, no! What do you want of me?

I swear to you I haven't lied to you !   I swear . . .
ugh !   [*He is choked.*]

ESSEX

Let him speak.   What do you swear ?

COURIER

My lord, I have not lied . . . I speak truth . . .

ESSEX

Tie him up.

COURIER

Let me speak . . .   I can . . . ugh . . .

ESSEX

Silence him.   We know too well what you have done,
sirrah.   We need no evidence of that.   What we ask
is that you tell us who set you on . . . and your ac-
complices.   Tell us this and I want no more of you.
You shall have your freedom . . . and this. . . [*He
tosses a clinking bag at his feet.*]   Speak.

COURIER

My lord, if I knew . . .

ESSEX

Bind him.   Truss him up and cut him open.   Dispense
with these niceties.   Have you no knife ?
[*He is bound.*]
We have heard enough !   Take out his tongue !
[*They approach him.   He becomes calm.*]

COURIER

My lord, I am not a coward, though it may seem to you

I am, for I have cried out . . . but I cried out
Not so much for pain or fear of pain
But to know this was Lord Essex, whom I have loved
And who tortures innocent men.

ESSEX

Come, silence him !

COURIER

Come then. I am innocent. If my lord Essex
Is as I have believed him, he will not hurt me;
If he will hurt me, then he is not as I
And many thousands believe him, who have loved him,
And I shall not mind much dying.
[*A pause.*]

ESSEX

Let him go.
[*They unbind the* COURIER.]
I thought my letters had been tampered with.
You'd tell me if it were so.

COURIER

My honored lord,
By all the faith I have, and most of it's yours,
I'd rather serve you well and lose in doing it
Than serve you badly and gain. If something I've
   done
Has crossed you or worked you ill I'm enough punished
Only knowing it.

ESSEX

This letter came
From the queen's hands ?

COURIER

It is as I received it
From the queen's hands.

ESSEX

There was no other?

COURIER

No other.

ESSEX

Take this and go.
[*He tosses the bag to the* COURIER.]

COURIER

I have brought misfortune . . .

ESSEX

You bring good news.   We break camp tomorrow for
London . . .   Go . . . take   that   news   with   you.
They'll welcome you outside.   Remain with my guard
and return with us.
[*The* COURIER *goes out.*]

MARVEL

We march tomorrow?

ESSEX

Yes.

MARVEL

Under orders?

ESSEX

No.
[*He reads.*]

"Lord Essex is required to disperse his men
And return to the capital straightway on his own
Recognizance, to give himself up."

MARVEL

And nothing with this?

ESSEX

Give out the necessary orders, we shall
Move at daybreak.

MARVEL

Yes, my lord.

ESSEX

And it is
As well it falls out this way! By right of name
And power and popular voice this is my kingdom . . .
This England under my feet, more mine than hers,
As she shall learn. It is quite as well.

MARVEL

There is no man
But will think so. There is victory in your path,
My lord. The London citizens will rise
At the first breath of your name.

ESSEX

Yes . . . that I'm sure of.

MARVEL

And with London in your hands . . . well . . . it's
   your world then . . .
As far as you like.

ESSEX

And I am glad for England.
She has lain fallow in fear too long ! Her hills
Shall have a spring of victory. Goodnight.

MARVEL

Goodnight.

ESSEX

And for this order, I received it not.
[*He tears the paper.*]

CURTAIN

ACT TWO

SCENE III

SCENE: *The council hall of Act I is cleared here for a court assembly. Those who attended the council are present, save for* ESSEX, *also the* FOOL, ELLEN, MARY, TRESSA, PENELOPE, BACON *and other* LORDS-AND-LADIES-IN-WAITING. BURGHLEY *and* CECIL *are standing to one side in earnest talk. Across from them a group made up of* RALEIGH, BACON, *the* FOOL *and a number of others.*

BURGHLEY

These players should be put down with an iron hand. They have neither conscience nor morals. They will make any display for money. In my young days they were allowed only interludes and instructive entertainment. The queen has been too lax . . .

CECIL

Have you seen this play of Richard II ?

BURGHLEY

I see no plays.

CECIL

It's high treason. Richard is deposed in it. High treason.

BACON

Treason to depose a king ?   Not if you succeed.

CECIL

No, but treason to teach treason.

BACON

What is treason ?

RALEIGH

Said jesting Pilate.

CECIL

Is it not treason to depose a king ?

RALEIGH

What if it makes a king of you ?

THE FOOL

It would then be treason not to have done it.

BACON

The Fool is a Jesuit.

THE FOOL

In truth, he was deposed.   It is treason to all his successors to deny it.

BACON

An excellent Jesuit.

THE FOOL

What ? I a Jesuit ? Jesu !

PENELOPE

And a wit.

BACON

Bad.

PENELOPE

Very bad.

RALEIGH

Unutterably bad. What ? Jesu-wit ! Poisonous !
Shall we allow this ?

PENELOPE

I am guilty. I surrender.

RALEIGH

What did you do with the body ?

PENELOPE

There was none. I did eat my words.

RALEIGH

A cannibal, a monster, a word-swallower !

THE FOOL

A man-eater.

PENELOPE

Nay, nay !

BACON

Do you eat your men with butter or salt ?

PENELOPE

With salt if they are buttery and with butter if they are salty.

RALEIGH

Ready then.   Here comes a salty man to be buttered.

PENELOPE

A butter-in.

THE FOOL

A salt-butter.

BACON

A cheese . . . a whole cheese.

TRESSA

Full of holes, holey.

ELLEN

Pitted.

PENELOPE

What ?   Am I pitted against a cheese ?

RALEIGH

Let but this cheese roll into your pit, lady . . . and you are answered.

PENELOPE

No . . . you are answered.   You are answered no.

BURGHLEY

[*To* CECIL] There can be no doubt the Essex faction sent money to the actors to purchase a performance of Richard.   It is an old play; it would draw no public.

CECIL

The actors are then accessory.

BURGHLEY

Think you so?

CECIL

They could hardly be unaware of the purposes of the Essex party.

BACON

Is it so certain that Essex has a purpose?

CECIL

He has led his army into London.

BACON

The men live in London.   Moreover the order to disperse on landing may not have been received.   Such things have happened.

CECIL

Yes?

BACON

Aye, indeed.

CECIL

[To BURGHLEY] You are to see these actors?

BURGHLEY

They are sending spokesmen today.

THE FOOL

Let them put on the play for us.

TRESSA

Yes . . . the deposition scene. It may convince us.
We may all turn rebel.

BURGHLEY

Tut !

THE FOOL

Tut ? What does this mean . . . this tut ?

BURGHLEY

Will you learn manners, sirrah ? In my young days
there was no such loose speaking about the court.

THE FOOL

There was no tutting, neither.

PENELOPE

You are mistaken. There used to be tutting parties.
They all brought their tutting.

THE FOOL

Fie on you ! Also pooh on you !

PENELOPE

Yes . . . there were fieing and poohing parties also.

RALEIGH

True, true. Well I remember the old days when all
the young people would get together and try which
could make the greatest pooh.

TRESSA

There was such laughter and jesting !

RALEIGH

Ah, yes, at the old Tut, Fie and Pooh Tavern ! It's torn down now, but what a place it was !

THE FOOL

The game went out of fashion, alas, when it was discovered that a virgin could always pooh farther than anybody else.

TRESSA

Tut !

MARY

Fie !

ELLEN

Pooh !

THE FOOL

I beg pardon. I had forgotten there were virgins present.

PENELOPE

We are all virgins.

RALEIGH

The proof then, quickly. Show me.

PENELOPE

It is nothing that can be seen, my lord.

RALEIGH

They say seeing is believing.

PENELOPE

Virginity is rather a state of mind.

ELLEN

Nay . . . a state of preservation.

THE FOOL

I have seen these preserved virgins.

RALEIGH

You have seen them ?

THE FOOL

Seen them ? I've been bothered by them. The whole court used to be driven indoors by them regularly on our progress through Middlesex.

RALEIGH

They are worse at night, I believe ? Middlesex . . . Middlesex . . .

PENELOPE

Change the subject, gentles. This virginity begins to wear thin.

THE FOOL

It has worn clear through, and a great hole appears in the center.

PENELOPE

A hole in your wit.

RALEIGH

His Jesuit.

PENELOPE

His half-wit.
[*A* HERALD *enters and speaks to* CECIL.]

THE HERALD

My lord, there are two fellows here who ask for audience with the queen.

CECIL

Who are they?

HERALD

Players, my lord.

CECIL

Tell them to wait. The queen will see them presently. [*The* HERALD *goes out.*]

BURGHLEY

To my mind it was one of these same players writ the ballad that was posted up at St. Paul's.

CECIL

No, no . . . the man has been discovered . . . and will have his ears cropped for it.

BURGHLEY

But he could not have written it . . . he was but an instrument. The actors are too devilish ingenious at writing ballads. I cannot put it out of my mind they are all treasonous scoundrels.

RALEIGH

Is this the ballad on the Earl's return?

CECIL

Aye . . . "When England needeth victories
         She calleth Essex on . . . "

And more to the same purpose. What I cannot understand is that the queen should take no steps to put the city in a posture of defense. Essex draws near with his army . . . and we swing the gates as usual.

BACON

Is that a symptom of danger . . . that an English general should return with his army to the English capital ?

CECIL

Are you not aware that Essex' house in the Strand is a camp brimming full of armed nobles going and coming ?

THE FOOL

It is much more likely to be brimming with drunken nobles going and coming brim full.

CECIL

Be quiet !

THE FOOL

Fool.
[CECIL *lays a hand on his sword angrily. The* FOOL *points to his own breast and repeats:*]
Fool.
[CECIL *turns away. There is a rustling among those present. Several rise. At the rear the* QUEEN *appears silently, two* LADIES *following her. She comes forward without speaking, her eyes seeking for someone. She fixes on* LORD BURGHLEY.]

THE QUEEN

Is it true, then, my dear Burghley, that you have taken
to attending the Theatre ?

BURGHLEY

No, madam.

THE QUEEN

It was not you, then, who forbade the performances of
Richard II without asking my advice ?

BURGHLEY

It was, madam.

THE QUEEN

On what ground ?

BURGHLEY

Your Majesty, the play is treasonous. It shows the
deposition of a king, and its performance was procured
by rebels.

THE QUEEN

Rebels ?   What rebels ?

BURGHLEY

I know not, madam. I have sent for the players to
discover that.

THE QUEEN

You have sent for them ?

BURGHLEY

Aye, madam . . . and they are here.

THE QUEEN

They will laugh at you, dear Burghley.

BURGHLEY

Others have laughed at me, Majesty.

THE QUEEN

They will laugh at you, sir, and you will deserve it. Is my kingdom so shaky that we dare not listen to a true history ? Are my people so easily led that the sight of a king deposed in play will send them running thither to pull the queen out of her chair ? Have we not passion plays in every little town showing the murder of our Lord ? You are nervous, Lord Burghley. Let these children play their plays.

CECIL

Your Majesty, I very much fear they are not all children, and that they mean to do harm.

THE QUEEN

Then let them. Let them do all the harm they can. Are we too stupid to see that to prohibit a rebellious play is to proclaim our fear of rebellion ? Who is there here who fears a rebellion against me ? I do not.

CECIL

It is dangerous to let these mutterings grow, dear queen.

ELIZABETH

It is dangerous to touch them. Let them mutter, if they will. Let them cry out . . . let them run the

streets, these children ! When they have worn themselves weary running and crying "Up with Essex !"
"Down with Elizabeth !" and got themselves drunk on
mutual pledges, they will go to bed and sleep soundly
and wake up wiser. Let me speak to these players.
Bring them to me.

BURGHLEY

Here, madam ?

ELIZABETH

Here.

CECIL

Majestas, adsunt legati de curia Galliæ. Placetne eos
recipere antequam . . .

THE QUEEN

Cras illos recipiam.

CECIL

Sed maxime præstat . . .

THE QUEEN

Si bene mihi videbitur, cras redituros recipiam !
Nay, I can bang you in Latin too !
[CECIL *goes out.* ELIZABETH *sits and turns to the*
FOOL.]
You, sirrah . . . I hear that you have fallen in love.
Do you wish to be whipped ?

THE FOOL

I would rather have been whipped, madam; much
rather.

ELIZABETH

Why ?

THE FOOL

It would hurt less.

ELIZABETH

Good. You shall be whipped.

THE FOOL

Madam, if you can whip it out of me I will give you my
lucky shilling.

ELIZABETH

You shall be whipped and keep your shilling.

THE FOOL

You would better take it, madam queen.

ELIZABETH

Your shilling?

THE FOOL

Yes, madam queen, to buy another whip with for yourself. Nay, you had perhaps better buy several. But
in truth, dear queen, I have not fallen in love, only a
pretty little strumpet has fallen in love with me and I
beg leave that we be allowed to marry.

ELIZABETH

Is she of the court?

THE FOOL

Yes, madam.

ELIZABETH

What, are there strumpets at court?

THE FOOL

Oh, they are all strumpets here at court. Some are here because they are strumpets and some are strumpets because they are here, but strumpets they all are.

ELIZABETH

Which is it you wish to marry ?

THE FOOL

It is not that I wish to marry her, madam, but she wishes to marry me. [*Walking about to choose, finally pointing to* TRESSA] This one, Majesty.

TRESSA

[*Leaping at him*] Scoundrel ! . . .

THE FOOL

[*Pointing to* ELLEN] No, no . . . I mean this one.

ELLEN

You dog ! You . . .
[*The* FOOL *passes* PENELOPE *by.*]

THE FOOL

[*Pointing to* MARY] Or that one . . .

MARY

What !

THE FOOL

I feel sure it was one of them, Majesty . . . but it was dark at the time . . . and in truth I gave her my word of honor in the dark that I would make an honest woman of her by daylight. It is thus that most marriages are made.

ELIZABETH

How, fool ?

THE FOOL

In the dark, my lady.   Quite in the dark.

ELIZABETH

[*To a soldier*] Take this fool, captain, and put him
in the dark for three days with but little bread and
water.   I have a distaste for this fooling.

THE FOOL

No, no, madam.

ELIZABETH

I am tired of your strumpets !   And let him not see his
lady Penelope meanwhile.   You will be sure of that,
mistress ?

PENELOPE

I have no desire to see him.

ELIZABETH

Whom do you desire to see ?

PENELOPE

No-one, your Majesty.

ELIZABETH

You lie !   This Mistress Gray, take her too !   Let her
have bread and water !   [*She looks at* PENELOPE *with
hatred.*]

PENELOPE

Your Majesty . . . what is this ?

ELIZABETH

I am weary to death of you! I am weary of all men and women, but more of you than any! You have written. You have had letters! I say, take her out of my sight!

[*The soldiers start to take out* PENELOPE *and the* FOOL.]

Whip them first, whip them both!

[*The two are taken to the door.*]

Nay, leave them here, leave them, knaves . . . leave them! Damn you, do you hear me! You are too quick to obey orders! You like this whipping too well, sirrah! You have an itch for laying on! You beef-witted bastards! And now let us have entertainment, gentle lords! Let us be merry! The players are here! Let us have a play!

[*A* HERALD *runs in to the queen without ceremony, calling out as he comes.*]

THE HERALD

Your Majesty, Your Majesty! Lord Scroop sends me from the city to tell you there is a rising in London! There is a mob rising in the city!

ELIZABETH

What . . . is this one of the players? Are you playing Richard II for us?

THE HERALD

No, no, Your Majesty! A great number of people came through Fleet Street . . . and they have sacked a grocer's and broken into a wine-merchant's cellar! It is said they will break into Fleet Prison and set all free. . .

ELIZABETH

Not they. If they've broken into a wine-cellar they'll get no farther. We're a marvellous people, we English, but we cannot hold liquor. Now if they were Scotch one might worry. What are they saying, these wine drinkers ?

THE HERALD

I cannot tell you that, Your Majesty.

ELIZABETH

Are they not crying "Up with Essex !" "Down with Elizabeth !" ?

THE HERALD

Yes, madam !

ELIZABETH

Why surely. What else would they be crying ? "Up with Essex !" Viva ! "Down with Elizabeth !" A bas ! The queen is dead, long live the king ! If I were there I would cry it myself ! It has a marvellous ring ! "Up with Essex !" "Down with Elizabeth !"

BURGHLEY

What are we to do, madam ?

ELIZABETH

[*To the* HERALD]
What is the Lord Mayor doing about this ?

HERALD

Nothing, Madame.

ELIZABETH

How like a Lord Mayor and how sensible. That's the first principle of government. Never do anything. Let the others make all the mistakes.

CECIL

But madam . . . there are five hundred of the royal guard at the Tower. . .

ELIZABETH

Let the mayor of London look out for his people. If he allows them to run up and down breaking into wine-cellars, it's his own affair.

BURGHLEY

But if it spreads to the palace, Majesty?

ELIZABETH

Why yes . . . let them bring their revolution here to me. I should be amused to see it. They are children, Burghley, drunken children. Would you fire on children?

BURGHLEY

Then let me go into London, madam . . .

ELIZABETH

And call out the guard and put down these traitors with powder and ball? No! They are to be allowed to get quite drunk and then go to sleep. Where are these players?

[CECIL *enters with* BURBAGE *and* HEMMINGS.]

CECIL

Here, madam.

ELIZABETH

Ah, yes, bold Burbage and handsome Hemmings. Well, my masters, I understand that you have come to me to have your noses slit and your thumbs branded ? Is it so ?

BURBAGE

Only if unavoidable, Your Majesty.

ELIZABETH

You have put on a play, I believe ?

BURBAGE

Many, Your Majesty.

ELIZABETH

You have revived the old play of Richard II, including in it the deposition scene which was censored on its first presentation, and you have done this to foster treasonous projects.

BURBAGE

No, Your Majesty, I swear it.

ELIZABETH

You have not played this play ?

BURBAGE

But not to foster treason, that I swear.

ELIZABETH

If you played Richard with that pot-belly it was treason indeed. Then for what purpose ?

BURBAGE

To make money.

ELIZABETH

On an old play?

BURBAGE

We were paid in advance. . .

ELIZABETH

By whom?

BURBAGE

By Lord Southampton.

BURGHLEY

You see? A friend of Essex.

ELIZABETH

You have much too handsome a nose for slitting, Master Hemmings, yet you say nothing.

HEMMINGS

There is only this to say, Your Majesty . . . that we knew nothing of any traitorous intent in the matter . . . and that, had we known of such intent, we would not have given the performance.

ELIZABETH

I think you are all traitorous knaves and rascals, as a matter of fact, in league with Essex and Southampton and the smoothest liars in Christendom. Is there something in this?

HEMMINGS

No, madam.

ELIZABETH

You know Essex and Southampton ?

HEMMINGS

We know Lord Southampton.

ELIZABETH

How much were you paid for the revival of Richard ?

HEMMINGS

Three pounds, Your Majesty.

ELIZABETH

No more ?

HEMMINGS

No more.

ELIZABETH

Play it again this afternoon, masters, play it at my request this afternoon, and you shall have ten pounds for it. Lord Cecil, pay Master Burbage ten pounds from the royal exchequer for one performance of Richard. And let it stand in the record.

CECIL

Yes, madam.

ELIZABETH

[*To* HEMMINGS] And tell Lord Southampton when you see him that I paid ten to his three. Will you tell him ?

HEMMINGS

Yes, Your Majesty.

ELIZABETH

And when you have all this treason out of your systems

be ready to play Sir John Falstaff for me at the end
of the week.   I should like to see your Falstaff again,
sir.

BURBAGE

Yes, Your Majesty.

ELIZABETH

You may go.
[BURBAGE *and* HEMMINGS *go out.*]

CECIL

[*Waiting till they are gone*]
You are mad, Your Majesty!   This is a rebellion, and
you play into their hands.   The outer court is throng-
ing with messengers from the city!   Half the town is
in uprising!

ELIZABETH

I know.

CECIL

Madam . . .

ELIZABETH

Little man, little man, let me alone.

CECIL

This much I must tell you.   Lord Essex has been seen
with an armed force in the city.

ELIZABETH

Lord Essex?

CECIL

With an army.   Where he is now no-one can say.

ELIZABETH

And if one were to guess?

CECIL

He is on his way hither.

ELIZABETH

So I think.   I shall be glad to see him.   Let him bring his revolution here.   How long think you it will last after I have looked on it ?

BURGHLEY

Madam, the palace is unprotected from the waterside. The guard must be drawn up.

ELIZABETH

With your permission, my lord, I would rather not.

CECIL

I took the liberty of ordering a guard posted along the river.

[*A door is opened without and a sudden snarl of angry voices breaks in on the conference.*]

THE VOICES

"Who has given these orders ?"
"Back there . . . back !"
"Not the queen, by God !"
"The queen . . . the queen !   Defend the queen !"
"An Essex !"
"Hold your mouth !"
"Stand back, fellow !"

ESSEX

[*Outside*] I say the queen will see me !   Stand back ! [*There is a clank of armor in the hallway and* ESSEX *appears in the doorway, soldiers following him.*]

ELIZABETH

You come with a file of soldiers at your back, my lord
of Essex.

ESSEX

Do I need them, Your Majesty ?

ELIZABETH

No.

ESSEX

Then be off with you. Follow my orders. . . They
told me you would not see me.

ELIZABETH

They were wrong. I will see you. It seems you are
   in rebellion,
My good lord.   Enter and state your grievance,
If you have grievance.   For myself, I have
A great affection for rebels, being one myself
Much of the time.

ESSEX

I am no rebel, Your Majesty . . .
But, newly arrived from Ireland, and bearing news
Of your subjects there, I venture to come to see you,
No more.

ELIZABETH

And your army ? . . . You have an army with you ?

ESSEX

I have brought my men home to London.

ELIZABETH

You received
My orders, no doubt, directing you to disband ?

ESSEX

I believed them to be mistaken. To disband on the
coast
And leave my expedition there, seemed strange,
And dangerous to the country. An army turned loose
Becomes a mob.

ELIZABETH

And you tell me this ! You are informed in these matters
But I am not !

ESSEX

Indeed, that is quite true . . .
I do know about armies . . . and you do not.

ELIZABETH

Oh, yes . . .
Oh, indeed. And who paid them then ? I believe
Your supplies were cut off ?

ESSEX

I have paid them.

ELIZABETH

They are then
In your service ?

ESSEX

In my service and therefore
Devoted yours.

ELIZABETH

And Ireland ?   How of Ireland ?

ESSEX

I could have conquered Ireland had you given me time.
I left it worse than I found it.

ELIZABETH

An honest answer,
At any rate.

ESSEX

Why should I lie ?   The fault,
If any, was yours.   To conquer Ireland requires
More than the months you gave me.   Years, perhaps.

ELIZABETH

You were engaged in subduing the rebels, then,
When I summoned you home ?

ESSEX

Just so.

ELIZABETH

You were not, by chance,
Joined with the rebels ?

ESSEX

Never.

ELIZABETH

You held no parleys
With our friend Tyrone ?

ESSEX

I did.   They were part of my plan.

ELIZABETH

Your plans! Your plans! Why did you write me
    nothing
Of these your plans? Am I a witch to find out
What happens on the far side of the Irish Sea
Without being told?

ESSEX

I wrote you . . .

ELIZABETH

Masterly letters,
Brief, to the point, wasting no words, in short,
Nothing.

ESSEX

I know not what Your Majesty means
By that. I wrote you fully, and in answer
Received no reply.

ELIZABETH

You wrote me?

ESSEX

Many times.

ELIZABETH

And had no letters from me?

ESSEX

None.

ELIZABETH

Before God,
If the couriers were tampered with there shall be
Some necks stretched here! My lords, I wish to speak
With Lord Essex here alone! Leave us.

CECIL

Dear queen,
Do you think it safe . . .

ELIZABETH

Leave us !
[BURGHLEY *makes a sign and the stage is silently emp-
tied save for the* QUEEN *and* ESSEX. *A pause.*]
What did you write me ?

ESSEX

I wrote you my love — for I thought you loved me
    then —
And then I pled with you not to bring me home
In the midst of my mission — and then at last angrily —
For I had not heard — but always to say I loved you —
Always.

ELIZABETH

But is this true ?

ESSEX

Would I lie ?

ELIZABETH

Some one
Has lied and will pay with his life if this is true ! —
Before God and hell — Some one will pay for this.

ESSEX

What did you write me ?

ELIZABETH

I wrote — my love —
God keep you safe — I know not — and then, not hear-
    ing,
I wrote God knows what madness — as to a rebel —

Thinking you no longer mine — faithless !
Thinking —

ESSEX

I would I had known — I was in torment —
I — forgive me —

ELIZABETH

You should never have gone away.
God, how I've hated you ! —

ESSEX

No !

ELIZABETH

Planned to put you to torture !

ESSEX

I have been in torture !
[*He steps toward her.*]

ELIZABETH

Not yet — I can't breathe yet — I can't breathe —
Or think or believe —

ESSEX

Nor I.

ELIZABETH

Can we ever —
Believe again ?   Can it be as it used to be ?

ESSEX

We can make it so.

ELIZABETH

Come, kill me if you will.   Put your arms round me —
If you love me.   Do you still love me ?

ESSEX

Yes.

ELIZABETH

Yes, yes —
If this were false, then, then truly — then I should die.
I thought because I was older — you see — some one
    else —

ESSEX

No one — never a breath —

ELIZABETH

Is it all, all as before ?

ESSEX

We have not changed.

ELIZABETH

No.   Yes, a little, perhaps.
They have changed us a little.

ESSEX

Not I.   I have not changed.

ELIZABETH

Can I trust you now ?

ESSEX

Sweet, think back, all those months,
All those hideous months !   No word, no love.
And when word did come, it was to make me prisoner !
Christ, I have pride !
And though I came here in defiance, I came truly to
    find you
Who have been lost from me.

ELIZABETH

Do you ask forgiveness ?
It is all forgiven.

ESSEX

Then, why then, hell's vanished —
And here's heaven risen out of it, a heaven of years
In the midst of desolate centuries.

ELIZABETH

We have so few years.
Let us make them doubly sweet, these years we have,
Be gracious with each other, sway a little
To left or right if we must to stay together —
Never distrust each other — nay, distrust
All others, when they whisper. Let us make this our
    pact
Now, for the fates are desperate to part us
And the very gods envy this happiness
We pluck out of loss and death.

ESSEX

If two stand shoulder to shoulder against the gods,
Happy together, the gods themselves are helpless
Against them, while they stand so.

ELIZABETH

Love, I will be
Your servant. Command me. What would you have ?

ESSEX

Why nothing —

ELIZABETH

Take this my world, my present in your hands !
You shall stand back of my chair and together we
Shall build an England to make the old world wonder
And the new world worship ! — What is this doubt in
   your brow ?

ESSEX

I am troubled to be dishonest.   I have brought my army
Here to the palace — and though it's all true what we've
   said —
No letters — utter agony over long months —
It is something in myself that has made me do this,
Not Cecil — nor anyone.   No one but myself.
The rest is all excuse.

ELIZABETH

Speak what you will.

ESSEX

If you had but shown anger I could have spoken
Easily.   It's not easy now, but speak I must !
Oh, I've thought much about this
On lonely marches and in distant tents,
Thinking of you and me.   I say this now
Without rancor — in all friendliness and love —
The throne is yours by right of descent and by
Possession — but if this were a freer time,
And there were election, I should carry the country be-
   fore me,
And this being true, and we being equal in love,
Should we not be equal in power as well ?

ELIZABETH

We are equal.
I have made you so.

ESSEX

Yes, but still it's all yours —
Yours to grant me now or take away.

ELIZABETH

How could this well be otherwise ?

ESSEX

Am I not — and I say this too in all love —
As worthy to be king as you to be queen ?
Must you be sovereign alone ?

ELIZABETH

You are young in policy,
My Essex, if you do not see that if I
Should grant high place to you now it would show ill
   to the kingdom —
It would be believed that you had forced this on me,
Would be called a revolution.   It would undermine
All confidence.   What is built up for years
In people's minds blows away like thistledown
When such things get abroad.

ESSEX

But is this your reason
Or have you another ?   Would you trust me as king ?

ELIZABETH

No.

ESSEX

And are you still reluctant to give up
Your prerogatives ?

ELIZABETH

Yes.

ESSEX

Then now, when the country is mine, the court in my
   hands,
You my prisoner, I must send my men away,
Disband my army, give back your kingdom to you,
And know I have been king for a moment only
And never will be again ?

ELIZABETH

I am your prisoner ?

ESSEX

The palace and the city are in my hands.
This England is mine now for the taking —

ELIZABETH

This is your friendship !   This is your love !

ESSEX

As water finds its level, so power goes
To him who can use it, and soon or late the name
Of king follows where power is.

ELIZABETH

Oh, my Essex,
You are a child in war as you are in council.
Why all this talk of power ?   No army opposed you
When your troops came the road from Ireland.   No
   guard was set

To stop your entrance with your thousand halberds.
Shall I tell you why ?   Because I wished to keep
A semblance of peace between us.   And for that,
I am your prisoner !

ESSEX

Yes.   My dear prisoner.

ELIZABETH

Now I do know at least
What it was you wanted.   You wanted my kingdom.
    You have it.
Make the best of it.   And so shall I.
What are your plans ?

ESSEX

I have none.

ELIZABETH

The Tower, the block —
You could hardly take a queen prisoner and have no
    thought
Of her destiny.   I am my mother's daughter,
I too can walk the path my mother walked.

ESSEX

These are heroics.   You know you are free as air.

ELIZABETH

If I do as you ask.

ESSEX

Is it so hard to share your power with your love ?
I could have all — and I offer to share with you.

ELIZABETH

Let's have no more pretending.
I'd have given all — but you came with an army, de-
    manding —
In short, you don't love — nor trust me — no — nor
    want me —

ESSEX

God knows I have wanted you.   I have wanted power —
Believed myself fitted to hold it — but not without you.

ELIZABETH

If you had wanted me would you rise and strike
At me with an army ?   Never, never !   You'd have
    come
To me quietly, and we'd have talked of it together
As lovers should — and we'd both have our way —
And no one the wiser.   But now, to take the palace,
Hold me prisoner — no — what you wanted you've
    taken —
And that is all you shall have.   This is your kingdom —
But I — I am not yours.

ESSEX

But I am yours
And have been.

ELIZABETH

Who will believe that ?   Not the world,
No, and not I.   I'd rather go to the Tower
Than share my place on terms like these.   Put me
    where I
Will do least harm.

ESSEX

I cannot, could not, will not.

ELIZABETH

If I could have given freely —
But not now.   Not surrendering.   Not to a victor.

ESSEX

I am no victor if I lose you.   The only gift
That I could take from you, is that we are equals.

ELIZABETH

Yes, but not now.

ESSEX

I ask one word from you.
Give me this word — this one word — and these soldiers
Shall leave, and you shall be free.

ELIZABETH

I'll believe that
When it happens.

ESSEX

I'll believe you when you promise.

ELIZABETH

Then you have my promise.
You shall share the realm with me.   As I am queen,
I promise it.

ESSEX

Then this is my answer.
[*He kisses her, then calls.*]
Marvel ! — Marvel !
[MARVEL *enters.*]

Carry out the order of release.   Dismiss my guard —
Return the palace into the queen's hands.
Retire with all our forces to the Strand.
Release all prisoners.   Release the queen's guard
And send them to their stations.
[MARVEL *goes out.*]
The palace will be
Returned as quickly as taken.   This is our last quarrel.

ELIZABETH

Yes — our last.

MARVEL'S VOICE

[*Off-stage*]
Form for retire !

ANOTHER VOICE

Form for retire !

A MORE DISTANT VOICE

Form for retire !

A VOICE

[*In the distance.*]
Ready to march !

ANOTHER VOICE

Ready to march !

ANOTHER

All ready !

ANOTHER

Ready, captain !
[MARVEL *enters.*]

MARVEL

The order is obeyed, my lord.

ESSEX

Follow your men.

MARVEL

Yes, my lord.
[*He goes out.*]

ESSEX

It is as I planned.   They are leaving the palace.
Now let us talk no more of this tonight —
Let us forget this matter of thrones and kingdoms
And be but you and me for a while.

ELIZABETH

[*Immobile.*]
Yes — yes —
Let us forget.   Have you kept your word indeed?

ESSEX

I have kept my word.

ELIZABETH

If I clapped my hands
Would my guard come now — or yours?

ESSEX

Yours only.   Shall I call them?

ELIZABETH

No — I'll call them.
[*She claps her hands four times.   Captain Armin appears in the entrance followed by four Beef-eaters with halberds.   They stand at attention in the entrance.*]
To be sure I have a guard

Once more.

[*To the* CAPTAIN.]

The palace has been returned ?   It is in
Our hands ?

CAPTAIN

Yes, Majesty.

ELIZABETH

I have ruled England a long time, my Essex,
And I have found that he who would rule must be
Quite friendless, without mercy, without love.
Arrest Lord Essex !
Arrest Lord Essex !   Take him to the Tower
And keep him safe.

ESSEX

Is this a jest ?

ELIZABETH

I never
Jest when I play for kingdoms, my lord of Essex.

ESSEX

I trusted you.

ELIZABETH

I trusted you,
And learned from you that no one can be trusted.
I will remember that.

ESSEX

Lest that should be all
You ever have to remember, Your Majesty,
Take care what you do.

ELIZABETH

I shall take care.

[ESSEX *unsheathes his sword, breaks it across his knee, flings it at the foot of the throne, turns and walks out between the two files of guards.*]

CURTAIN

ACT THREE

SCENE: *The queen's apartments in the Tower, a square and heavy room, long and with a raised stone platform at one end of which stands a regal chair. It is dawn, the light filtering in coldly. ELLEN stands in the doorway at the left, weeping, with one arm before her face. THE FOOL, who has been sleeping wrapped in the draperies of the queen's chair, uncoils himself from among them and rolls over to rub his eyes. TRESSA hurries in.*

TRESSA

Come back quickly, dear, quickly! She's sorry she hurt you. She'll have no one else read to her.

ELLEN

[*Weeping*] I can't read now. I'm — I don't mind if she strikes me — only — it wasn't my fault — We're all so weary.

TRESSA

She's sorry —

THE FOOL

[*Waking*] One, two — there should be three.
[MARY *comes to the door.*]

MARY

[*Very low*] Ellen —

THE FOOL

Three.

MARY

Ellen ! She wants you at once.
[ELLEN *runs out.*]

THE FOOL

Where am I ?

MARY

Yes — and what are you doing there ?

THE FOOL

Trying to sleep.

MARY

Sleep ? In the Tower ?

THE FOOL

Come and help me. I have heard that you are perfect
at lying down.
[MARY *and* TRESSA *go out.* THE FOOL *looks about him
sleepily, then remembers something and hunts for it under a chair. When he extracts it it proves to be a roasted
bird on a wooden platter, covered with leaves. He ex-
amines it, then replaces a large leaf over it.* PENELOPE,
fully dressed, comes in from the rear.]
Penelope ?

PENELOPE

Yes ?

THE FOOL

Have you slept ?

PENELOPE

No.

THE FOOL

Then you should break your fast.   You are hungry?

PENELOPE

No.   I can't eat.

THE FOOL

[*Showing his capon*] Look.

PENELOPE

What's that?

THE FOOL

Breakfast.   I brought it from Whitehall.

PENELOPE

Eat it then.   [*She sits on a step disconsolately.*]

THE FOOL

You won't have any?

PENELOPE

No.

THE FOOL

[*Pushing the food away*] I'm not hungry either.

PENELOPE

Eat it, poor fool.

THE FOOL

I don't want it.   I brought it for you.

PENELOPE

I know. But eat it. [*She wipes her eyes.*]

THE FOOL

Why should you weep?

PENELOPE

God knows. He never wept for me.

THE FOOL

The earl's not dead yet, remember.

PENELOPE

No.

THE FOOL

And she'll never let it happen.

PENELOPE

The clock's struck five. He's to die at six.

THE FOOL

Why has she not sent to him?

PENELOPE

She has. We were awake all night. She has sent messages but he's not answered. She's been waiting for word from him. But he's as silent as if he wanted to die.

THE FOOL

Will she let them kill him if he says nothing?

PENELOPE

She's a strange woman. She wants him to beg her pardon . . . or something like that.

THE FOOL

Would you beg her pardon if you were he?

PENELOPE

No.

THE FOOL

Then he won't. For I think he's as proud as you.

PENELOPE

He has not said a word or sent a message since his arrest.

THE FOOL

And the queen has not slept?

PENELOPE

No.

THE FOOL

Nor you?

PENELOPE

No.

THE FOOL

God help these women.

PENELOPE

She says she gave him a ring once. If he ever wanted
forgiveness he was to send the ring. And he sits there
stubbornly with the ring on his finger. Oh, God, will
nothing happen?
[*The* FOOL *has absent-mindedly pulled the capon
toward him again, and begins to eat.* ELIZABETH
emerges from the rear.]

ELIZABETH

Penelope ?

PENELOPE

Yes.

ELIZABETH

Have the players come ?

PENELOPE

Not yet.
[*The* FOOL *has pushed the food guiltily behind him.*]

ELIZABETH

These cheating grooms ! I'll have them carbonadoed
for this dallying ! I shall go mad here ! Bring me
the little book of prayers . . . from the window-sill.
No . . . leave it. The gods of men are sillier than
their kings and queens . . . and emptier and more
powerless. There is no god but death, no god but
death !
[*She sees the food the* FOOL *has been hiding.*]
Gnaw your bones somewhere else !
[*The* FOOL *goes out left.*]
Come here, my dear. I heard the clock strike five.

PENELOPE

Yes. I heard it.
[*They sit together on the steps, and* PENELOPE *puts
her arm round* ELIZABETH.]

ELIZABETH

Do you love him well, my dear ?

PENELOPE

Yes, Your Majesty.
[ELIZABETH *bows her head wearily on* PENELOPE.]

ELIZABETH

I love him.   He has never loved me.

PENELOPE

Yes, yes.   He does love you.   I've been madly jealous
of you.

ELIZABETH

Of me ?   Poor child.

PENELOPE

But he loved you . . . and never me at all.

ELIZABETH

How do you know ?

PENELOPE

He told me.

ELIZABETH

What did he say ?

PENELOPE

He said, "I love her dearly."   I wanted him for myself, and I warned him against you.   He laughed at me.
He said, "I love her very dearly."

ELIZABETH

You tell me this because you want to save him.

PENELOPE

No, dear queen.   It's true.

ELIZABETH

This is the end of me, dear.   This is the end.
It comes late.   I've been a long while learning,
But I've learned it now.   Life is bitter.   Nobody
Dies happy, queen or no.   Will he speak, think you ?
Will he send to me ?

PENELOPE

No.   Not now.

ELIZABETH

You see,
This is the end of me.   Oh, I shall live,
I shall walk about and give orders . . . a horrible
    while . . .
A horrible old hag.

PENELOPE

You must send for him.
He's proud as you are, and you have the upper hand.
He'll say nothing.   You must send for him, bring him
    here.
[*The chimes ring the quarter hour.*]

ELIZABETH

Not yet.   Not yet.
[*She rises.*]
Where are the players ?   I sent
For the players hours ago !   They shall pay for this,
The   insolent   servants !   Mary . . . Tressa,   God's
    head !
I'm bestially served !   Ellen !

[ELLEN *looks in, partly dressed.*]
Find out if the players
Are here?   And be quick.

ELLEN

Yes, madam.
[*She disappears.*]

ELIZABETH

Where's my fool?

THE FOOL

[*Looking in with a bone in his hand.*]
Here, madam.

ELIZABETH

Where are you when I need you?
Look at the oaf!   Say nothing!   You're funny enough
The way you are with your capon in your mouth!
Eat!   Eat!   Let me see you!

THE FOOL

I don't seem to be hungry!

ELIZABETH

Eat, I say!

THE FOOL

Yes, madam.
[*He tries to eat.*]

ELIZABETH

Now wipe your fingers.
Here, take my napkin, child.   Come here!   You're
    disgusting!

[*She gives him a kerchief.*]
Can you not clean your face ?

THE FOOL

With this ?

ELIZABETH

Aye, with that.
[*She takes his bone and throws it.*]
Why do you make mouths at it ?   It's clean.

THE FOOL

Yes, madam !
[*He begins to wipe his mouth, then starts to cry, and
sitting down on the step, sobs heavily, his head in his
hands.*]

ELIZABETH

What is it now ?   What good's a fool that cries
When you need comfort ?   What's the matter ?

THE FOOL

Please,
I don't know.   You aren't like the queen.

ELIZABETH

I am
The queen, though.

TRESSA

[*Looking in*]
The players, madam.

ELIZABETH

Bring them here.

PENELOPE

The time's grown short.   Will you send for him ?

ELIZABETH

Wait . . . he may come.

PENELOPE

No, no.   He won't.   You'll let it go too long
Watching the players.

ELIZABETH

Let them come in.
[TRESSA *is seen at the doorway with the actors.*]

PENELOPE

You should eat
A little something first.

ELIZABETH

No, no.   Bring them in.
[*The* ACTORS *enter.*]
Come in, my masters, let us have a play . . .
Let us have revels and amusements quickly . . .
If ever you played play now.   This is my bad
Quarter of an hour.

PENELOPE

Please, please . . .

ELIZABETH

Quick !   Quick . . .
You are late, sirs . . . never mind . . . some scene
   from Falstaff . . .

The one where he lies to the prince about running away
And the prince catches him . . .

HEMMINGS

Where, Majesty ?

ELIZABETH

There, anywhere. Come, sit down. Sit down.
[*The girls and the* FOOL *group about her.*]
Begin, Falstaff ! "I call thee coward ! I'll see thee
Damned ere I call thee coward !"

FALSTAFF

I call thee coward ! I'll see thee damned ere I call
thee coward: but I would give a thousand pound I
could run as fast as thou canst.

PRINCE HENRY

What's the matter ?

FALSTAFF

What's the matter ! there be four of us here have ta'en
a thousand pound this day morning.

PRINCE HENRY

Where is it, Jack ? where is it ?

FALSTAFF

Where is it ! taken from us it is: a hundred upon poor
four of us.

PRINCE HENRY

What, fought ye with them all ?

FALSTAFF

All! I know not what ye call all; but if I fought not
with fifty of them, I am a bunch of radish: if there
were not two or three and fifty upon poor old Jack,
then am I no two-legged creature.

ELIZABETH

Come, come . . . this is not to the purpose . . . I had
thought this witty . . .
[*The players pause.*]
Play! Play!

PRINCE HENRY

Pray God, you have not murdered some of them.

FALSTAFF

Nay, that's past praying for: I have peppered two of
them; two I am sure I have paid, . . . two rogues in
buckram suits. I tell thee what, Hal, . . . if I tell
thee a lie, spit in my face, call me horse. Thou knowest my old ward . . . here I lay, and thus I bore my
point. Four rogues in buckram let drive at me . . .

PRINCE HENRY

What, four? thou saidst but two even now.

FALSTAFF

Four, Hal; I told thee four.

POINS

Ay, ay, he said four.

FALSTAFF

These four came all a-front, and mainly thrust at me.
I made me no more ado but took all their seven points
in my target, thus.
[*The* QUEEN *walks from place to place, restlessly.*]

PRINCE HENRY

Seven ? why, there were but four even now in buckram.

POINS

Ay, four in buckram suits.

FALSTAFF

Seven, by these hilts, or I am a villain else.

PRINCE HENRY

Pr'ythee, let him alone; we shall have more anon.

FALSTAFF

Dost thou hear me, Hal ?

PRINCE HENRY

Ay, and mark thee too, Jack.

ELIZABETH

Aye, aye . . . we are listening . . .
Play !

FALSTAFF

Do so, for it is worth the listening to.   These nine in
buckram that I told thee of . . .

PRINCE HENRY

So, two more already.

FALSTAFF

Began to give me ground: but I followed me close, came in foot and hand; and with a thought seven of the eleven I paid.

PRINCE HENRY

O monstrous ! eleven buckram men grown out of two !

FALSTAFF

But, as the devil would have it, three misbegotten knaves in Kendal green came at my back and let drive at me . . . for it was so dark, Hal, that thou couldst not see thy hand.

PRINCE HENRY

These lies are like the father that begets them . . . gross as a mountain, open, palpable.   Why, thou clay-brained guts, thou nott-pated fool, thou whoreson, obscene, greasy tallow-ketch . . .

FALSTAFF

What, art thou mad ? art thou mad ? is not the truth the truth ?

PRINCE HENRY

Why, how couldst thou know these men in Kendal green, when it was so dark thou couldst not see thy hand ? come, tell us your reason: what sayest thou to this ?

POINS

Come, your reason, Jack . . . your reason.

FALSTAFF

What, upon compulsion ?   Give a reason on compulsion ! if reasons were as plenty as blackberries I would give no man a reason on compulsion, I.

PRINCE HENRY

I'll be no longer guilty of this sin; this sanguine coward, this bed-presser, this horse back-breaker, this huge hill of flesh . . .

FALSTAFF

Away, you starveling, you elf-skin, you dried neat's tongue . . . O for breath to utter what is like thee ! . . . you tailor's yard, you sheath, you bow-case, you vile standing-tuck . . .

PRINCE HENRY

Well, breathe awhile, and then to it again: and when thou hast tired thyself in base comparisons, hear me speak but this.

POINS

Mark, Jack.

PRINCE HENRY

We two saw you four set on four; you bound them, and were masters of their wealth. . . Mark now, how a plain tale shall put you down. . . Then did we two set on you four; and, with a word, out-faced you from your prize, and have it: yes, and can show it you here in the house: . . . and, Falstaff, you carried your guts away as nimbly, with as quick dexterity, and roared for mercy, and still ran and roared, as ever I heard bull-calf. What a slave art thou, to hack thy sword as thou hast done, and then say it was in fight ! What trick, what device, what starting-hole, canst thou now find out to hide thee from this open and apparent shame ?

POINS

Come, let's hear, Jack; what trick hast thou now ?

FALSTAFF

By the Lord, I knew ye as well as He that made ye. Why, hear ye, my masters: was it for me to kill the heir-apparent ? Should I turn upon the true prince ? Why, thou knowest I am as valiant as Hercules: but beware instinct; the lion will not touch the true prince. Instinct is a great matter; I was a coward on instinct. I shall think the better of myself and thee during my life; I for a valiant lion, and thou for a true prince. But, by the Lord, lads, I am glad you have the money. What, shall we be merry ? Shall we have a play extempore ?

ELIZABETH

My God, my God . . . can one not forget for a moment ?
Who are these strangers ? What is this interlude ?
Go ! Go ! It's a vile play and you play it vilely !
Go ! By my God, will no-one deliver me from this torment ?
[*The players start out.*]
Take your trappings and go !
[*They leave. The chimes strike.*]

Again . . . the half-hour . . .
[CECIL *enters*.]
Yes ?
[*To* PENELOPE]
Was I not wise to wait ?   He has spoken first !   Yes ?

CECIL

Your Majesty, a citizen rabble has gathered
To protest the execution of Essex.   The captain
Begs permission to use your guard.   There's no other
Force at hand to disperse them.

ELIZABETH

It's your day, Cecil.
I daresay you know that.   The snake-in-the-grass
Endures, and those who are noble, free of soul,
Valiant and admirable . . . they go down in the
    prime,
Always they go down . . .

CECIL

Madam, the guard
Is needed at once . . .

ELIZABETH

Aye . . . the snake-mind is best . . .
One by one you out-last them.   To the end
Of time it will be so . . . the rats inherit the earth.
Take my guard.   Take it.   I thought you brought
    word from . . .
Go, call Lord Essex for me

From his cell . . . and bring him thither ! I'll wait
no longer !

CECIL

Lord Essex is prepared for execution.
The priest has been sent to him.

ELIZABETH

Bring him here, I say,
And now . . . at once !
[CECIL *bows and goes out.*]
Go out from me, all of you,
All save Penelope. Go quickly, quickly . . .
All . . .
[*They leave.*]
Penelope, bring my robe, the one
Laid out . . .
[PENELOPE *goes.* ELIZABETH *seats herself in the royal
chair.* PENELOPE *returns with the robe.*]
Look here in my face, Penelope. He's so young,
And I'm old, girl, I'm old. It shows in my eyes.
Dear, you're so young. Do not be here when he
comes . . .
Do you mind ? You'll look so young.

PENELOPE

Yes, madam . . . but you . . .
You're beautiful.

ELIZABETH

Beautiful still ? But I was once . . . I was . . .
You'd not believe it now.

PENELOPE

Oh, yes . . .
You're always beautiful.   You've always been.

ELIZABETH

Thank you,
My dear.   Go now.   He'll come.

PENELOPE

Yes.
[*She goes out to the rear.   After a moment* ESSEX
*enters from the left with a Guard.   The Guard leaves
him and steps out.*   ESSEX *is dressed in black and is
very pale.*]

ESSEX

You sent for me ?
Or so they said.

ELIZABETH

Yes.

ESSEX

It would have been kinder
To leave me with my thoughts till the axe came down
And ended them.   You spoil me for death.

ELIZABETH

Are you
So set on dying ?

ESSEX

I can't say I care for it.
This blood that beats in us has a way of wanting
To keep right on.   But if one is to die
It's well to go straight toward it.

ELIZABETH

You must have known
I never meant you to die.

ESSEX

I am under sentence
From Your Majesty's courts.   There's no appeal that
   I know of.
I am found guilty of treason on good evidence,
And cannot deny it.   This treason, I believe,
Is punishable with death.

ELIZABETH

God knows I am proud . . .
And bitter, too . . . bitter at you with much cause,
But I have sent for you.   I've taken the first step
That way.   Do not make me take the next !

ESSEX

The next is to the scaffold.   It's only a step
Now, and I've made ready.

ELIZABETH

Aye, you are bitter,
Too; we have let it go late; we've both
Waited for the other.   But it was I who spoke
First . . . Will you make me tell you first how much
I've longed for you ?   It's hard for me.

ESSEX

My dear,
You can tell me so gracefully, for you
Have nothing to gain or lose by me . . . but I

Have life and love to gain, and I find it less
Than fitting to speak like a lover, lest you suppose
I do it to save my head.

ELIZABETH

It's true that you never
Loved me, isn't it ?   You were ambitious, and I
Loved you, and it was the nearest way to power,
And you took the nearest way ?   No, no . . . one mo-
    ment . . .
This is an hour for truth, if there's ever truth . . .
I'm older than you . . . but a queen; it was natural
You'd flatter me, speak me fair, and I believed you.
I'm sorry I believed you.   Sorry for you
More than for me.

ESSEX

Why, yes . . . that's true enough.
Now may I go ?   This dying sticks in my mind,
And makes me poor company, I fear.

ELIZABETH

It was true.
It was true then ?

ESSEX

If you wish to make me tell you
What you well know, how much I used to love you,
How much I have longed for you, very well, I will
    say it.
That's a small victory to win over me now,
But take it with the rest.

ELIZABETH

You did love me?

ESSEX

Yes.

ELIZABETH

And love me still?

ESSEX

Yes.   You should know that, I think.

ELIZABETH

You kept my ring.   You never sent my ring.
I've been waiting for it.

ESSEX

You may have it back
If you have use for it . . . I had thought to wear it
As far as my grave, but, take it.

ELIZABETH

I'd have forgiven
All that had passed, at any hour, day or night,
Since I last saw you.   I have waited late at night
Thinking, tonight the ring will come, he will never
Hold out against me so long, but the nights went by
Somehow, like the days, and it never came,
Till the last day came, and here it is the last morning
And the chimes beating out the hours.

ESSEX

Dear, if I'd known . . .
But I could not have sent it.

ELIZABETH

Why ?

ESSEX

If I'd tried
To hold you to a promise you could not keep
And you had refused me, I should have died much more
Unhappy than I am now.

ELIZABETH

I'd have kept my promise.
I'd keep it now.

ESSEX

If I offered you this ring ?

ELIZABETH

Yes . . . even now.

ESSEX

You would pardon me, set me free,
Cede back my estates to me, love me as before,
Give me my place in the state ?

ELIZABETH

All as it was.

ESSEX

And what would happen to your throne ?

ELIZABETH

My throne ?
Nothing.

ESSEX

Yes, for I'd take it from you.

ELIZABETH

Again ?
You'd play that game again ?

ESSEX

The games one plays
Are not the games one chooses always.   I
Am still a popular idol of a sort.
There are mutterings over my imprisonment,
Even as it is . . . and if you should set me free
And confess your weakness by overlooking treason
And setting me up in power once more, the storm
That broke last time would be nothing to the storm
That would break over you then.   As for myself,
I played for power and lost, but if I had
Another chance I think I'd play and win.

ELIZABETH

Why do you say this ?

ESSEX

I say it because it's true.
I have loved you, love you now, but I know myself.
If I were to win you over and take my place
As it used to be, it would gall me.   I have a weak-
     ness
For being first wherever I am.   I refuse
To take pardon from you without warning you

Of this.   And when you know it, pardon becomes
Impossible.

ELIZABETH

You do this for me ?

ESSEX

Why, yes,
But not altogether.   Partly for England, too.
I've lost conceit of myself a little.   A life
In prison's very quiet.   It leads to thinking.
You govern England better than I should.
I'd lead her into wars, make a great name,
Perhaps, like Henry Fifth and leave a legacy
Of debts and bloodshed after me.   You will leave
Peace, happiness, something secure.   A woman governs
Better than a man, being a natural coward.
A coward rules best.

ELIZABETH

Still bitter.

ESSEX

Perhaps a little.
It's a bitter belief to swallow, but I believe it.
You were right all the time.
[*The chimes ring three-quarters.*]
And now, if you'll pardon me,
I have an appointment near-by with a headsman.
He comes sharp on the hour.

ELIZABETH

You have an hour yet.
It's but struck five.

ESSEX

It struck five some time since.

ELIZABETH

It cannot go this way !

ESSEX

Aye, but it has.
It has and will. There's no way out. I've thought
   of it
Every way. Speak frankly. Could you forgive me
And keep your throne ?

ELIZABETH

No.

ESSEX

Are you ready to give
Your crown up to me ?

ELIZABETH

No.   It's all I have.
[*She rises.*]
Why, who am I
To stand here paltering with a rebel noble !
I am Elizabeth, daughter of a king,
The queen of England, and you are my subject !
What does this mean, you standing here eye to eye
With me, your liege ?   You whom I made, and gave
All that you have, you, an upstart, defying
Me to grant pardon, lest you should sweep me from
   power

And take my place from me ?   I tell you if Christ his
    blood
Ran streaming from the heavens for a sign
That I should hold my hand you'd die for this,
You pretender to a throne upon which you have
No claim, you pretender to a heart, who have been
Hollow and heartless and faithless to the end !

ESSEX

If we'd met some other how we might have been
    happy . . .
But there's been an empire between us ! I am to
    die . . .
Let us say that . . . let us begin with that . . .
For then I can tell you that if there'd been no empire
We could have been great lovers.   If even now
You were not queen and I were not pretender,
That god who searches heaven and earth and hell
For two who are perfect lovers, could end his search
With you and me.   Remember . . . I am to die . . .
And so I can tell you truly, out of all the earth
That I'm to leave, there's nothing I'm very loath
To leave save you.   Yet if I live I'll be
Your death or you'll be mine.

ELIZABETH

Give me the ring.

ESSEX

No.

ELIZABETH

Give me the ring.   I'd rather you killed me
Than I killed you.

ESSEX

It's better for me as it is
Than that I should live and batten my fame and fortune
On the woman I love. I've thought of it all. It's better
To die young and unblemished than to live long and rule,
And rule not well.

ELIZABETH

Aye, I should know that.

ESSEX

Is it not ?

ELIZABETH

Yes.

ESSEX

Goodbye, then.

ELIZABETH

Oh, then I'm old, I'm old !
I could be young with you, but now I'm old.
I know now how it will be without you.   The sun
Will be empty and circle round an empty earth . . .
And I will be queen of emptiness and death. . .
Why could you not have loved me enough to give me
Your love and let me keep as I was ?

ESSEX

I know not.
I only know I could not.   I must go.

ELIZABETH

[*Frozen*]
Yes.
[*He goes to the door.*]
Lord Essex !
[*He turns.*]
Take my kingdom. It is yours !
[ESSEX, *as if not hearing, bows and goes on.* PENEL
OPE *runs in, meeting him.*]

PENELOPE

My lord ! She has forgiven you ?

ESSEX

Goodbye, my dear.
[*He kisses her.*]

PENELOPE

No, no ! She loves you ! Go to her.
[ESSEX *goes out.*]
Run to her ! She waits you still ! See, if you turn
She waits you still ! Dear queen, would you let him
 go ?
He goes to his death ! Send, send after him !
[*The* QUEEN *lifts her head and shows a face so stricken
that* PENELOPE, *who has gone to her, says no more.
The clock strikes six.* ELIZABETH *bows her head on*
PENELOPE'S *knees, her hands over her ears.*]

CURTAIN